Dare to **wake up** to **younger looking skin.**

Anew Retinol Recovery Complex.
The breakthrough Retinol technology for dramatically younger looking skin. Overnight, a patented delivery system enables pure Retinol to work gently within the skin's surface, so fine lines and wrinkles visibly diminish, age spots seem to fade. Start to see results in as little as two weeks or your money back. Guaranteed. Dare to change your mind about Avon. Call your Avon Representative, visit Avon at http://www.avon.com or order direct

1-800-FOR-AVON

A V O N

SIMPLE goodness

Front cover: Sweet Onion-Smothered Hamburger, page 42; Oven Fries, page 65; photography by Howard L. Puckett; styling by Cathy Muir.

Editor: **Alyson Moreland Haynes**

Graphic Designer: **Amy Heise**

Managing Editor: **Kay Fuston**

Senior Writer: **Melissa Chessher Aspell**

Copy/Production Editor: **Liz Rhoades**

Copy Editor: **Carol Boker**

Photographers: **Ralph Anderson, Jim Bathie, Howard L. Puckett**

Photo Stylists: **Cindy Manning Barr, Kay E. Clarke, Virginia R. Cravens, Cathy Muir**

Weight Watchers Magazine Test Kitchen Director: **Kathleen Phillips**

Editor, *Weight Watchers* Magazine: **Kate Greer**

Art Director: **Austin Davis**

Editorial Coordinator: **Christine O'Connell**

Editorial Assistant: **Joe Watts**

Senior Vice President, Publisher: **Jeffrey C. Ward**

General Manager: **Thomas C. Marshall**

Business Manager: **Michael W. Stern**

Production Manager: **Brent Kizzire**

Franchise Relations Manager: **Betsey Hummel**

President and CEO: **Tom Angelillo**

Executive Vice President: **Bruce Akin**

Executive Vice President: **Scott Sheppard**

Vice President, Administration: **Jeanetta Keller**

Vice President, Consumer Marketing: **Hallett Johnson III**

Vice President, Circulation: **Pat Vander Meer**

Vice President, Magazine Production: **Larry Rinehart**

Financial Director: **Bruce Larson**

Back cover: Almond-Mocha Parfaits, page 81; photography by Howard L. Puckett; styling by Cindy Manning Barr.

WELCOME

Some of you may think "simple goodness" sounds redundant. Surely, anything simple must be good: a walk in the woods, a techno-colored gerbera daisy, a laugh. It is a fashionable notion: Everyone, it seems, is looking to simplify life as well as to make it more healthy. A similarly spirited phenomenon is the look back to foods that were common to our childhood dinner table: macaroni and cheese, mashed potatoes, meatloaf, and homemade breads. Lovingly called comfort foods, these dishes deliver emotional snapshots from an easier time. They also offer a welcome culinary respite from intricate dishes of the past few years: salads and desserts whose architecture and composition rival the Empire State Building and include pretty (though pointless) dustings, sprinkles, and drizzles around the plate.

But the connection between simplicity and good-for-you isn't so clear when it comes to food (as anyone who knows the nutritional analysis of Grandma's biscuit can attest). But a better, more positive angle is that many of the things that bolster our health are the most basic. Namely, fruits, vegetables, and grains. The philosophy of this cookbook is to use the latest nutritional information in combination with the best low-fat cooking techniques to compose a collection of recipes that is familiar, uncomplicated, flavorful, and, most important, healthy.

Translating "healthy" into physical data can be difficult. Each recipe in this cookbook includes the standard nutritional information: serving size, calories, protein, fat, carbohydrates, fiber, cholesterol, iron, sodium, and calcium. In addition to that analysis, recipes also include Selections and *POINTS*™, the basis for following the Weight Watchers 1•2•3 Success™ Weight Loss Plan. *POINTS* are calculated from a formula based on calories, fat, and fiber that assigns higher *POINTS* to higher-calorie, higher-fat foods. For example, fruits and vegetables are low in *POINTS* while a slice of pizza is high. (See the highlighted box below for *POINT* values for some common foods.) For more information about the 1•2•3 Success Weight Loss Plan and the Weight Watchers meeting nearest you, call 1-800-651-6000.

Whether you count *POINTS,* Selections, calories, or fat grams, use the seven Weight Watchers Guidelines for Healthy Living each day: 1) consume a variety of foods, 2) include two servings of milk products, 3) eat at least five servings of fruits and vegetables, 4) pay attention to serving sizes, 5) limit refined sugars and alcohol, 6) drink six or more glasses of water, and 7) do at least 20 minutes of physical activity.

Alyson M. Haynes

Sample Food Points

Broccoli	0
Carrots	0
Corn, 5-inch ear	1
Orange	1
Banana	2
Bagel, 1 small	3
Yogurt, plain fat-free	3
Pizza, 5-ounce slice	8
Grilled cheese sandwich	13

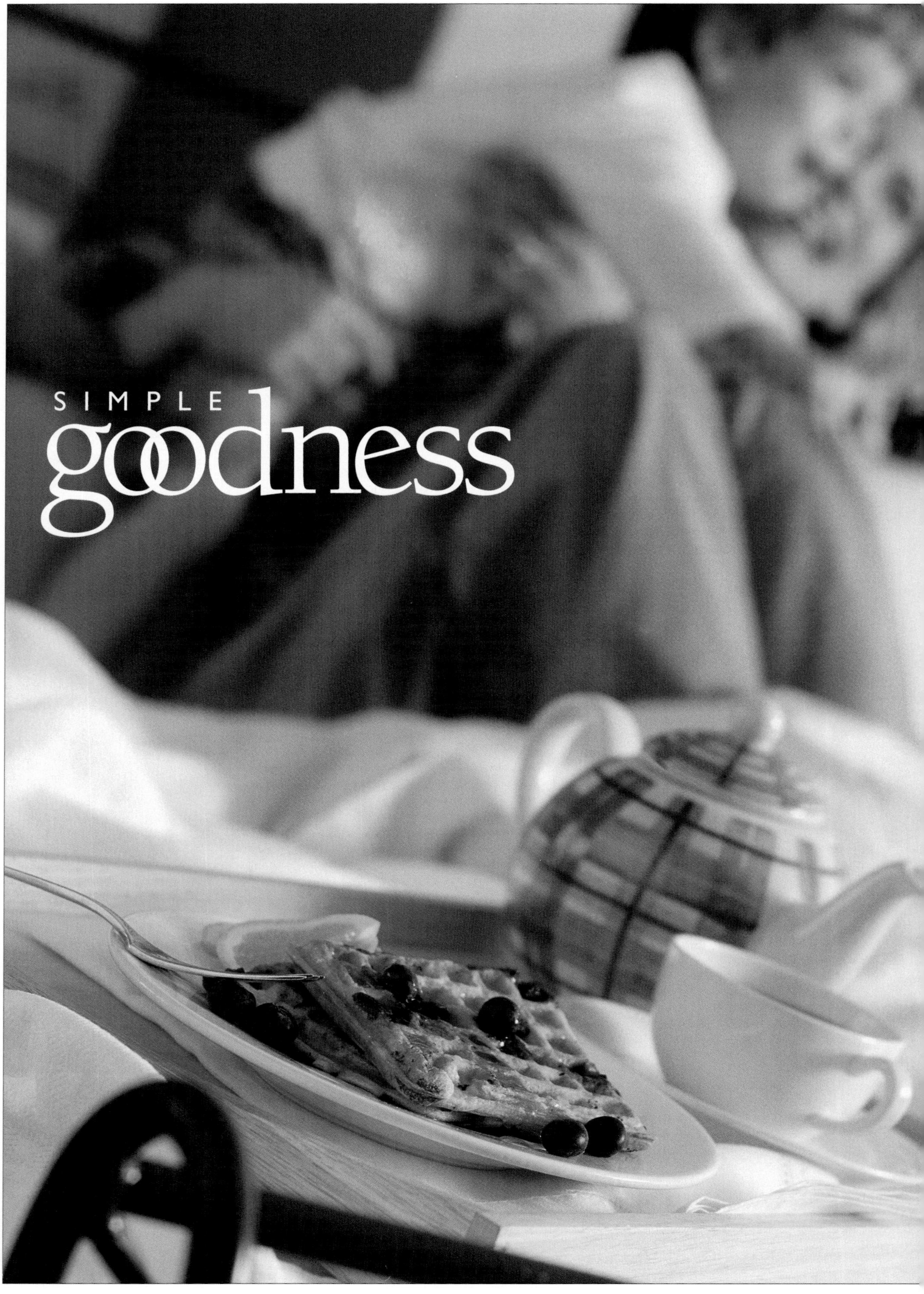
SIMPLE
goodness

c o n t e n t s

Page **9**

44

Page **51**

 55

85

Page **70**

Like Manna From Heaven

THESE EASY, HEALTHY BREADS
ARE A DIVINE ADDITION TO ANY TABLE.

*A*s unlikely as it seems, scientists have quantified and sanctified many of the things our grandmothers held as truths but were never considered worthy of a laboratory, a beaker, a white jacket. Hugs can heal. Prayer works. Eat your vegetables; they're good for you. Add to that list comfort foods, grain-based things like breads known for their ability to lift a down mood. Scientists discovered that carbohydrate-rich foods are not only healthy but contain higher levels of an amino acid called tryptophan, a building block of serotonin. And serotonin helps relieve the sourness of depression and irritability.

Grandmother didn't know about serotonin. But she knew breads and that the correct yeast roll just might erase a lost game, a failed test, a blue day. The recipes that follow operate on that theory but improve upon it by using shortcuts and quick tricks to reduce the time in the kitchen without losing any of the flavor or texture: a Mexican salsa bread, cheesy dinner sticks, and a yeast bread that requires no kneading. Because, as Grandma will surely attest, even a good roll won't take the edge off too many hours in a hot kitchen.

Crisp-and-Spicy Cheese Twists and Mexican Salsa Bread

isp-and-Spicy Cheese Twists

e a pizza cutter to cut strips more easily.

- cup grated Parmesan cheese
- teaspoon paprika
- teaspoon ground red pepper
- (10-ounce) can refrigerated pizza crust dough
- tter-flavored cooking spray

Preheat oven to 425°.

Combine first 3 ingredients in a small bowl; well, and set aside.

Unroll pizza dough, and roll into a 12- x 8- ch rectangle. Lightly coat surface of dough with oking spray, and sprinkle with 2 tablespoons eese mixture. Fold dough in half to form an 8- -inch rectangle. Roll dough into a 12- x 8-inch ctangle. Lightly coat surface of dough with oking spray, and sprinkle with remaining eese mixture. Using fingertips, press cheese xture into dough.

Cut dough into 16 (8-inch-long) strips. ently pick up both ends of each strip, and ist dough. Place twisted strips of dough ½ ch apart on a large baking sheet coated with oking spray.

Bake at 425° for 8 minutes or until lightly owned. Remove twists from pan, and let cool wire racks. Yield: 16 breadsticks (serving size: readstick).

ections: 1 B; **Points:** 1
 serving: CAL 68 (15% from fat); PRO 2.7g; FAT 1.1g (sat 0.5g); RB 11.9g; FIB 0.6g; CHOL 1mg; IRON 0.3mg; SOD 189mg; LC 25mg

exican Salsa Bread

- cup (4 ounces) shredded reduced-fat Monterey Jack cheese, divided
- cup picante sauce
- cup chopped fresh cilantro
- (1-pound) Italian cheese-flavored pizza crust (such as Boboli)

Preheat oven to 350°.

Combine ½ cup cheese, picante sauce, and lantro in a small bowl; stir well. Spread over zza crust, and sprinkle with remaining cheese.

Place on a baking sheet, and bake at 350° for 15 minutes or until cheese melts. Cut into wedges. Yield: 8 servings (serving size: 1 wedge).

Selections: 2 B, 40 C; **Points:** 3
Per serving: CAL 143 (31% from fat); PRO 8.9g; FAT 4.9g (sat 2.2g); CARB 16.3g; FIB 0.1g; CHOL 13mg; IRON 0.4mg; SOD 520mg; CALC 122mg

Whole-Wheat Banana Muffins

1	cup all-purpose flour
1	cup whole-wheat flour
¼	cup toasted wheat germ
1	teaspoon baking powder
1	teaspoon baking soda
½	teaspoon salt
1⅓	cups mashed ripe banana (about 3 large)
⅔	cup sugar
¼	cup vegetable oil
1	large egg, lightly beaten

Cooking spray

1. Preheat oven to 350°.

2. Combine first 6 ingredients in a large bowl; make a well in center of mixture. Combine banana, sugar, oil, and egg; add to dry ingredients, stirring just until moist.

3. Divide batter evenly among 16 muffin cups coated with cooking spray. Bake at 350° for 20 minutes. Remove from pans immediately; let cool on a wire rack. Yield: 16 muffins (serving size: 1 muffin).

Selections: 1 B, 1 FA; **Points:** 3
Per serving: CAL 148 (% from fat); PRO 2.8g; FAT 4.4g (sat 0.7g); CARB 25.6g; FIB 2.1g; CHOL 14mg; IRON 0.8mg; SOD 157mg; CALC 22mg

VARIATION:

Whole-Wheat Banana Loaf

Preheat oven to 400°. Prepare batter as directed. Spoon batter into a 9- x 5-inch loaf pan coated with cooking spray. Bake at 400° for 40 minutes or until a wooden pick inserted in center comes out clean. Yield: 16 servings (serving size: 1 slice).

Raisin-Applesauce Bran Muffins

1½ cups shreds of wheat bran cereal (such as All Bran)
¾ cup unsweetened applesauce
½ cup low-fat buttermilk

Flour goes through a process called bolting (or sifting) at the mill, so additional sifting for most baked goods is not necessary.

However, flour tends to settle in the bag during shipping, so it's a good idea to stir the flour before spooning it into a measuring cup and leveling it off. On the other hand, cake flour and all-purpose flour used for delicate cakes and pastries should be sifted to ensure that the texture of the cake is light and airy.

¼ cup firmly packed brown sugar
¼ cup egg substitute
2 tablespoons vegetable oil
1¼ cups all-purpose flour
2 teaspoons baking powder
¼ teaspoon salt
½ teaspoon ground cinnamon
¾ cup raisins
Cooking spray

1. Preheat oven to 400°.

2. Combine first 3 ingredients in a bowl; stir well. Let stand 5 minutes. Stir in sugar, egg substitute, and oil. Combine flour, baking powder, salt, and cinnamon in a large bowl; make a well in center of mixture. Add cereal mixture, stirring just until dry ingredients are moist. Fold in raisins.

3. Divide batter evenly among 12 muffin cups coated with cooking spray. Bake at 400° for 20 minutes or until lightly browned. Remove from pans immediately; let cool on wire racks. Yield: 1 dozen (serving size: 1 muffin).

Selections: 1 B, 1 FR/V, 1 FA; **Points:** 2
Per serving: CAL 150 (19% from fat); PRO 3.9g; FAT 3.1g (sat 0.7g); CARB 31.5g; FIB 4.8g; CHOL 0mg; IRON 2.8mg; SOD 217mg; CALC 66mg

Lemon-Glazed Cranberry Rolls

1 (10-ounce) can refrigerated pizza crust dough
½ cup orange marmalade
⅔ cup dried cranberries
Cooking spray
½ cup sifted powdered sugar
1½ teaspoons lemon juice
1 teaspoon hot water

1. Preheat oven to 375°.

2. Unroll pizza dough, and pat into a 12- x 9-inch rectangle. Spread marmalade over dough, leaving a ½-inch border. Sprinkle cranberries over marmalade, pressing gently into dough. Beginning with a long side, roll up jelly-roll fashion; pinch seam to seal (do not seal ends of roll). Cut roll into 12 (1-inch) slices. Place slices, cut sides up, in muffin cups coated with cooking spray. Bake at 375° for 15 minutes or until golden. Remove rolls from pan, and place on a wire rack.

3. Combine powdered sugar, lemon juice, a hot water in a small bowl, stirring until smoo Drizzle icing over warm rolls. Yield: 1 doz (serving size: 1 roll).

Note: Substitute ⅓ cup apple jelly for the oran marmalade and ⅔ cup raisins for the cranberri if desired.

Selections: 1 B, 50 C; **Points:** 3
Per serving: CAL 155 (6% from fat); PRO 2.9g; FAT 1g (sat 0. CARB 34.7g; FIB 3g; CHOL 0mg; IRON 0.3mg; SOD 229mg; CA 15mg

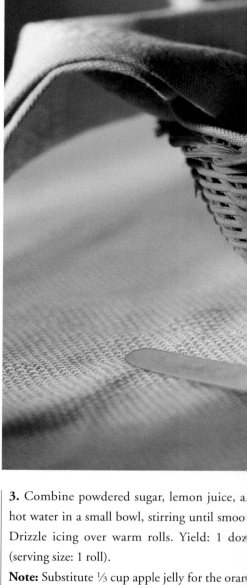

asy Drop Biscuits

2 cups all-purpose flour

  teaspoons baking powder

  teaspoon baking soda

  teaspoon salt

  cup plain low-fat yogurt

  cup egg substitute

  tablespoon vegetable oil

oking spray

Preheat oven to 400°.

Combine flour, baking powder, baking soda, and salt in a large bowl. Make a well in the center of the flour mixture. Combine low-fat yogurt, egg substitute, and vegetable oil; add yogurt mixture to dry ingredients, stirring just until moist.

3. Drop the dough by rounded tablespoons about 2 inches apart onto a baking sheet coated with cooking spray, and bake at 400° for 15 minutes or until golden. Yield: 1 dozen (serving size: 1 biscuit).

Try sweet Lemon-Glazed Cranberry Rolls with a cup of tea at brunch or as an afternoon snack.

yogurt, lemon rind, egg, and egg white; add to dry ingredients, stirring just until moist. Combine raspberries and 1 tablespoon flour, and toss gently to coat. Fold raspberries into batter. Spoon batter into a 6-cup Bundt pan coated with cooking spray. Bake at 350° for 45 minutes or until a wooden pick inserted in center comes out clean. Let cool in pan 10 minutes on a wire rack, and remove from pan. Let cool completely on a wire rack.

3. Combine powdered sugar and skim milk in a small bowl; stir well. Let stand 2 minutes. Drizzle glaze over cooled cake. Yield: 14 servings (serving size: 1 slice).

Selections: 1 B, 90 C; **Points:** 3
Per serving: CAL 169 (6% from fat); PRO 4.2g; FAT 1.2g (sat 0.3g); CARB 36.2g; FIB 2.2g; CHOL 17mg; IRON 1.3mg; SOD 86mg; CALC 58mg

Granola Muffins

3 cups low-fat granola with raisins
1 cup boiling water
2⅓ cups all-purpose flour
⅔ cup firmly packed brown sugar
2 teaspoons baking soda
¼ teaspoon salt
2 cups low-fat buttermilk
⅓ cup vegetable oil
1 large egg, lightly beaten
2 large egg whites, lightly beaten
Cooking spray

1. Preheat oven to 350°.

2. Combine granola and boiling water in medium bowl; let stand 10 minutes.

3. Combine flour, brown sugar, baking soda, and salt in a bowl; make a well in the center of mixture. Add buttermilk, vegetable oil, egg, and egg whites to granola mixture; stir well. Add the buttermilk mixture to dry ingredients, stirring just until moist.

4. Divide the batter evenly among 28 muffin cups coated with cooking spray. Bake at 350 for 20 minutes or until a wooden pick inserted in the center comes out clean. Remove the muffins from the pans immediately, and let coo

Raspberry Coffee Ring is packed with fresh berries and whole-grain goodness.

Selections: 1 B; **Points:** 2
Per serving: CAL 82 (18% from fat); PRO 3.1g; FAT 1.6g (sat 0.4g); CARB 13.5g; FIB 0.4g; CHOL 1mg; IRON 0.8mg; SOD 154mg; CALC 68mg

Raspberry Coffee Ring

1 cup all-purpose flour
1 cup firmly packed brown sugar
⅔ cup oat bran
½ cup whole-wheat flour
1 teaspoon baking soda
1¼ cups vanilla low-fat yogurt
½ teaspoon grated lemon rind
1 large egg, lightly beaten
1 large egg white, lightly beaten
1 cup raspberries
1 tablespoon all-purpose flour
Cooking spray
½ cup sifted powdered sugar
2 teaspoons skim milk

1. Preheat oven to 350°.

2. Combine first 5 ingredients in a large bowl, and make a well in center of mixture. Combine

wire racks. Yield: 28 muffins (serving size:
muffin).

ections: 1 B, 1 FA; **Points:** 3

serving: CAL 138 (25% from fat); PRO 3.3g; FAT 3.9g (sat
g); CARB 23.3g; FIB 1g; CHOL 8mg; IRON 1.1mg; SOD 128mg;
_C 27mg

sic Skillet Cornbread

 cups yellow cornmeal
 cup all-purpose flour
 teaspoons baking powder
 teaspoon baking soda
 teaspoon salt
 cups low-fat buttermilk
 tablespoons vegetable oil
 large egg, lightly beaten
 large egg whites, lightly beaten
 ooking spray

Preheat oven to 450°.

Combine first 5 ingredients in a large bowl;
ake a well in center of mixture. Combine but-
rmilk, oil, egg, and egg whites; add to dry ingre-
ents, stirring just until moist.

Place a 10-inch cast-iron skillet in a 450° oven
r 5 minutes or until hot. Remove skillet from
en; coat with cooking spray, and immediately
ur batter into hot skillet. Bake at 450° for 20
inutes or until lightly browned. Remove corn-
ead from skillet immediately. Yield: 10 servings
erving size: 1 wedge).

Selections: 2 B; **Points:** 3
Per serving: CAL 158 (18% from fat); PRO 5.8g; FAT 3.2g (sat
0.7g); CARB 26g; FIB 1.3g; CHOL 24mg; IRON 1.4mg; SOD
329mg; CALC 98mg

Blueberry Muffins

1¾ cups all-purpose flour
2   teaspoons baking powder
½   teaspoon ground allspice
¼   teaspoon salt
¾   cup skim milk
⅓   cup sugar
¼   cup vegetable oil
1   teaspoon grated lemon rind
1   teaspoon grated orange rind
1   teaspoon vanilla extract
1   large egg, lightly beaten
1   cup fresh or frozen blueberries, thawed
    and drained
Cooking spray

1. Preheat oven to 400°.

2. Combine first 4 ingredients in a medium
bowl; stir well. Make a well in center of mixture.
Combine milk and next 6 ingredients; add to dry
ingredients, stirring just until moist. Gently fold
in blueberries.

3. Divide batter evenly among 12 muffin cups
coated with cooking spray. Bake at 400° for 20
minutes or until golden. Remove from pans immediately; let cool on a wire rack. Yield: 1 dozen
(serving size: 1 muffin).

STEP BY STEP TO BLUEBERRY MUFFINS

Combine wet ingredients; add to dry ingredients.

Gently fold in blueberries.

Combine dry ingredients; stir well. Make a well in center of mixture.

Stir just until dry ingredients are moist.

Bake until a wooden pick inserted in center comes out clean.

Make-Ahead Directions:

Freeze muffins up to 2 weeks. Thaw at room temperature, or microwave 1 muffin at MEDIUM (50% power) 30 seconds or until warm.

Buttermilk Biscuits

1¾ cups all-purpose flour
2 teaspoons baking powder
½ teaspoon salt
½ teaspoon sugar
½ teaspoon baking soda
⅔ cup low-fat buttermilk
2 tablespoons vegetable oil
1 tablespoon fat-free sour cream
Butter-flavored cooking spray

1. Preheat oven to 400°.

2. Combine first 5 ingredients in a medium bowl; make a well in center of mixture. Combine buttermilk, oil, and sour cream, and add to dry ingredients, stirring just until dry ingredients are moist.

3. Turn dough out onto a lightly floured surface, and knead 5 or 6 times. Roll dough to a ¾-inch thickness; cut with a 2½-inch biscuit cutter. Place biscuits on a baking sheet; lightly coat tops of biscuits with cooking spray. Bake at 400° for 8 minutes or until lightly browned. Yield: 1 dozen (serving size: 1 biscuit).

Cinnamon-Raisin Biscuits

2 cups all-purpose flour
1½ tablespoons sugar
2 teaspoons baking powder
½ teaspoon ground cinnamon
¼ teaspoon salt
3 tablespoons chilled stick margarine, cut into small pieces
½ cup raisins
¾ cup 1% low-fat milk

½ cup sifted powdered sugar
1 tablespoon 1% low-fat milk

1. Preheat oven to 450°.

2. Combine first 5 ingredients in a bowl; cut in margarine with a pastry blender or 2 knives until mixture resembles coarse meal. Add raisins; toss well. Add ¾ cup milk; stir just until dry ingredients are moist.

3. Turn dough out onto a heavily floured surface; knead dough 4 or 5 times. Roll dough to a ½-inch thickness; cut with a 2½-inch biscuit cutter. Place on a baking sheet. Bake at 450° for 11 minutes or until golden.

4. Combine powdered sugar and 1 tablespoon of milk; stir well. Drizzle over the biscuits. Yield: 1 dozen (serving size: 1 biscuit).

> **N**othing quite compares with the enticing aroma of bread baking in the oven.

Date-and-Maple Scones

2 cups all-purpose flour
¼ cup firmly packed brown sugar
1½ teaspoons baking powder
½ teaspoon baking soda
¼ teaspoon salt
⅓ cup chilled stick margarine, cut into small pieces
½ cup chopped dates
½ cup 1% low-fat milk
3 tablespoons maple syrup
Cooking spray

1. Preheat oven to 400°.

2. Combine first 5 ingredients in a bowl; cut in margarine with a pastry blender or 2 knives until mixture resembles coarse meal. Add dates, and toss well. Combine milk and maple syrup. Add the milk mixture to dry ingredients, stirring just until dry ingredients are moist.

3. Turn dough onto a lightly floured surface; knead 4 or 5 times. Pat dough into an 8-inch

Cinnamon-Raisin Biscuits

SPOON, DON'T SCOOP, YOUR FLOUR

Baking is a science, especially low-fat baking. With less fat there is less room for error, particularly when measuring flour. Too much flour will most surely lead to a dry product. If you dip your measuring cup in a flour canister, you can overmeasure as much as ¼ cup more flour than if you lightly spoon it into the cup. So measure flour like this: Stir the flour several times with a fork to loosen and release any settling. Then, using a large spoon, spoon flour into the correct dry measuring cup until it is brimming over. Using a straight-edged spatula or knife, level the flour.

circle on a baking sheet coated with cooking spray. Cut dough into 12 wedges, cutting to but not through the dough (do not separate wedges).

4. Bake at 400° for 15 minutes or until scones are golden. Serve warm. Yield: 1 dozen (serving size: 1 scone).

Selections: 1 B, 1 FA; **Points:** 4
Per serving: CAL 176 (28% from fat); FAT 5.5g (sat 1.1g); PRO 2.7g; CARB 29.8g; FIB 1.2g; CHOL 0mg; IRON 1.3mg; SOD 168mg; CALC 61mg

Herbed Garlic Bread

¼ cup reduced-calorie stick margarine, softened
1½ tablespoons grated fresh Parmesan cheese
2 teaspoons minced fresh parsley
2 teaspoons minced fresh basil
¼ teaspoon garlic powder
12 (¾-inch-thick) slices French bread

1. Preheat oven to 400°.

2. Combine first 5 ingredients in a small bowl, and stir well. Spread mixture evenly over one side of each bread slice. Wrap bread in foil, and

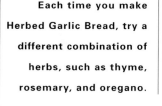

Each time you make Herbed Garlic Bread, try a different combination of herbs, such as thyme, rosemary, and oregano.

bake at 400° for 15 minutes. Yield: 12 serving

Selections: 1 B, 1 FA; **Points:** 2
Per serving: CAL 103 (26% from fat); PRO 2.6g; FAT 3g (sat 0 CARB 15.8g; FIB 0.7g; CHOL 1mg; IRON 0.6mg; SOD 203 CALC 14mg

No-Knead Tupperware Bread

3 packages dry yeast
3¾ cups warm water (105° to 115°)
10 cups all-purpose flour
6 tablespoons sugar
6 tablespoons stick margarine, melted
1 tablespoon salt
2 large eggs, lightly beaten
Cooking spray

1. Dissolve yeast in warm water in a 7-qu Tupperware container; let stand 5 minutes. A flour, sugar, margarine, salt, and eggs, stirri until well blended. Cover the container wit Tupperware lid, and seal. Let stand at ro temperature 1 hour or until lid "pops" off.

2. Spoon the dough evenly into 3 (9- x 5-in loaf pans coated with cooking spray. Cover and

CHOOSE YOUR CORNMEAL

Cornmeal is ground from dried corn kernels into one of three textures—fine, medium, or coarse. Coarse-ground or stone-ground cornmeal is more nutritious because this process retains some of the hull and germ of the corn. Unlike regular-ground cornmeal, stone-ground produces a cornbread with a coarse, slightly crunchy texture.

Depending on the type of corn used, cornmeal is either yellow, white, or blue. Yellow cornmeal has slightly more vitamin A than white, but all three colors of cornmeal can be used interchangeably in recipes. Look for blue cornmeal in specialty markets or the gourmet section of some super-markets. Another cornmeal, available in the South, is a product called self-rising cornmeal to which baking soda and salt have been added.

he dough rise in a warm place (85°), free from rafts, for 30 minutes or until doubled in bulk.

Preheat oven to 350°.

Bake at 350° for 40 minutes or until the aves sound hollow when tapped. Yield: 3 loaves, 6 servings per loaf (serving size: 1 slice).

elections: 1 B, 30 C; **Points:** 2
r serving: CAL 110 (16% from fat); PRO 2.9g; FAT 1.9g (sat 4g); CARB 20.1g; FIB 0.8g; CHOL 9mg; IRON 1.2mg; SOD 6mg; CALC 6mg

uttermilk Corn Sticks

cup yellow cornmeal
cup all-purpose flour
teaspoon baking powder
teaspoon baking soda
teaspoon salt
teaspoon paprika
cup low-fat buttermilk
tablespoons sugar
tablespoons vegetable oil
large egg, lightly beaten
Cooking spray

Preheat oven to 425°.

Combine cornmeal, flour, baking powder, aking soda, salt, and paprika in a medium owl; make a well in the center of mixture. Combine buttermilk, sugar, vegetable oil, and

egg; add to dry ingredients, stirring just until dry ingredients are moist.

3. Place cast-iron corn stick pans in a 425° oven for 5 minutes or until hot. Remove pans from oven; coat with cooking spray, and immediately pour batter into hot pans. Bake at 425° for 10 minutes or until lightly browned. Yield: 1 dozen (serving size: 1 corn stick).

Selections: 1 B, 1 FA; **Points:** 2
Per serving: CAL 88 (31% from fat); PRO 2.3g; FAT 3g (sat 0.6g); CARB 13g; FIB 0.5g; CHOL 19mg; IRON 0.7mg; SOD 124mg; CALC 39mg

Mom's Banana Bread

1   cup sugar
¼   cup light butter, softened
1⅔ cups mashed ripe banana (about 3 bananas)
¼   cup skim milk
¼   cup low-fat sour cream
2   large egg whites
2   cups all-purpose flour
1   teaspoon baking soda
½   teaspoon salt
Cooking spray

1. Preheat oven to 350°.

2. Combine sugar and butter in a bowl; beat at medium speed of a mixer until well blended. Add

Buttermilk Corn Sticks are the perfect accompaniment to a vegetable plate or bowl of soup.

Blueberry Waffles

nana, milk, sour cream, and egg whites; beat
ll, and set aside.

Combine flour, baking soda, and salt; stir well.
d dry ingredients to creamed mixture, beating
til blended.

Spoon batter into 4 (5- x 2½-inch) miniature
af pans coated with cooking spray. Bake at 350°
 45 minutes or until a wooden pick inserted in
nter comes out clean. Let cool in pans 10 min-
es on a wire rack; remove from pans. Let cool
mpletely on wire racks. Yield: 4 loaves, 4 serv-
gs per loaf (serving size: 1 slice).

ote: To make 1 (9-inch) loaf, spoon batter into
- x 5-inch loaf pan coated with cooking spray;
ke at 350° for 1 hour and 10 minutes. Yield: 1
af, 16 servings (serving size: 1 slice).

ections: 1 B; Points: 3
 serving: CAL 147 (14% from fat); FAT 2.2g (sat 1.4g); PRO
g; CARB 30.2g; FIB 1.1g; CHOL 7mg; IRON 0.8mg; SOD
mg; CALC 13mg

lueberry Waffles

4 cups all-purpose flour
  tablespoon baking powder
ash of salt
4 cups skim milk
  tablespoons vegetable oil
  large egg, lightly beaten
  large egg whites, lightly beaten
oking spray
  cup fresh or frozen blueberries
dditional blueberries (optional)

Combine first 3 ingredients in a medium
wl; stir well. Combine milk, oil, egg, and egg
ites in a small bowl; stir well. Add to flour
xture, stirring until well blended.

Coat a waffle iron with cooking spray, and pre-
at. Spoon about ⅓ cup of batter per waffle
to hot waffle iron, spreading batter to edges.
oon 2 tablespoons blueberries per waffle evenly
er batter. Cook 6 to 7 minutes or until steam-
g stops; repeat procedure with remaining batter
d blueberries. Serve with syrup. Garnish with
dditional blueberries, if desired. Yield: 8 (4-
ch) waffles (serving size: 1 waffle).

Note: If you are using frozen blueberries, do not
thaw them before adding to batter.

Selections: 1 B, 1 FA, 50 C; Points: 4
Per serving: CAL 189 (30% from fat); PRO 6.4g; FAT 6.3g (sat
1.2g); CARB 26.7g; FIB 1.6g; CHOL 29mg; IRON 1.6mg; SOD
86mg; CALC 176mg

Zucchini Bread

2   cups shredded zucchini
3   cups all-purpose flour
1¾ cups sugar
1   teaspoon baking soda
1   teaspoon salt
1   teaspoon ground cinnamon
¼   teaspoon baking powder
¾   cup applesauce
½   cup egg substitute
⅓   cup vegetable oil
1   tablespoon vanilla extract
Cooking spray

1. Preheat oven to 350°.
2. Place zucchini on several layers of paper towels; cover with additional paper towels. Let stand
5 minutes, pressing down occasionally. Set aside.
3. Combine flour and next 5 ingredients in a
large bowl; make a well in center of mixture.
Combine zucchini, applesauce, egg substitute,
oil, and vanilla; add to dry ingredients, stirring
just until moist.
4. Divide batter evenly between 2 (7½- x 3-inch)
loaf pans coated with cooking spray. Bake at 350°
for 1 hour and 15 minutes or until a wooden pick
inserted in center comes out clean. Let cool in
pans 10 minutes on a wire rack; remove from
pans. Let cool completely on wire rack. Yield: 2
loaves, 14 servings per loaf (serving size: 1 slice).

Selections: 1 B, 1 FA; Points: 3
Per serving: CAL 128 (20% from fat); PRO 1.9g; FAT 2.8g (sat
0.5g); CARB 23.9g; FIB 0.5g; CHOL 0mg; IRON 0.8mg; SOD
136mg; CALC 9mg

Brown Bread With Maple Cream

½   cup all-purpose flour
½   cup whole-wheat flour
½   cup yellow cornmeal
¼   cup rye flour
¾   teaspoon baking powder

BAKING AT HIGH ALTITUDES

High altitudes (above 3,500 feet) have a pronounced effect on baked goods. The atmospheric pressure at high altitudes is lower due to a thinner blanket of air. This decrease in air pressure means that adjustments need to be made in some ingredients, baking times, and baking temperatures.

• Decrease the amount of sugar used by approximately 1 teaspoon per tablespoon.

• Oven temperature may be decreased by 25°F to avoid adjusting baking time.

• Decrease the amount of yeast called for in the recipe by ½ teaspoon per tablespoon.

• As altitude increases, atmospheric pressure decreases, causing yeast breads to rise more rapidly. To extend the rising time and develop the characteristic flavor in yeast breads, allow the dough to rise twice, punching down the dough after each rising.

½   teaspoon salt
⅓   cup dried cranberries or raisins
1   cup low-fat buttermilk
⅓   cup molasses
½   cup maple syrup, divided
Cooking spray
1   (8-ounce) package Neufchâtel cheese

1. Combine first 6 ingredients in a large bowl; stir well. Stir in dried cranberries. Add buttermilk, molasses, and ⅓ cup maple syrup to dry ingredients, stirring just until moist. Pour batter into a 13-ounce coffee can heavily coated with cooking spray. Cover with aluminum foil; secure foil with a rubber band.

2. Place can on a shallow rack in a large, deep stockpot; add enough water to pot to come halfway up sides of can, and bring to a boil. Cover pot, and steam bread in boiling water for 2 hours, adding boiling water as needed.

3. Remove can from water; let bread cool in can on a wire rack for 10 minutes. Remove bread from can. Combine Neufchâtel cheese and remaining maple syrup; beat well with a mixer. Cut bread crosswise into 9 slices, and serve with Maple Cream. Yield: 9 servings (serving size: 1 slice bread and 1 tablespoon Maple Cream).

Selections: 1 B, 120 C; Points: 5
Per serving: CAL 245 (18% from fat); PRO 6.2g; FAT 4.8g (sat 2.7g); CARB 45.6g; FIB 2.1g; CHOL 16mg; IRON 1.9mg; SOD 310mg; CALC 127mg

Oatmeal-Buttermilk Pancakes

1¼ cups low-fat buttermilk
½   cup quick-cooking oats
½   teaspoon vanilla extract
1   tablespoon vegetable oil
1   large egg
1¼ cups all-purpose flour
2   tablespoons brown sugar
½   teaspoon baking soda
½   teaspoon salt

1. Combine first 3 ingredients in a small bowl; let stand 10 minutes, stirring occasionally. Stir in oil and egg.

2. Combine flour, sugar, baking soda, and salt in a large bowl; stir well. Add oat mixture to dry in-

gredients, stirring until well blended.

3. Spoon about ⅓ cup batter for each panc onto a hot nonstick griddle or nonstick ski Turn pancakes when tops are covered with b bles and edges look cooked. Yield: 8 panca (serving size: 2 pancakes).

Selections: 2 B, 1 FA, 70 C; Points: 6
Per serving: CAL 287 (22% from fat); PRO 10.1g; FAT 7g 2.1g); CARB 45g; FIB 2.1g; CHOL 55mg; IRON 2.5mg; S 509mg; CALC 116mg

Crumb-Topped French Toast

½   cup skim milk
½   teaspoon vanilla extract
¼   teaspoon salt
2   large eggs
1   cup cornflake crumbs
8   (1-ounce) diagonally cut slices French bread (about 1 inch thick)
¼   cup margarine, melted

1. Preheat oven to 450°.

2. Combine first 4 ingredients in a medi bowl; stir well with a whisk. Place cornfla crumbs in a shallow dish.

3. Dip bread slices into milk mixture, and dre in cornflake crumbs. Place bread slices on a b ing sheet, and drizzle with margarine. Bake 450° for 15 minutes or until golden brow Yield: 8 servings (serving size: 1 bread slice).

Selections: 1 B, 2 FA, 30 C; Points: 5
Per serving: CAL 212 (32% from fat); PRO 5.8g; FAT 7.6g 1.7g); CARB 29g; FIB 0.8g; CHOL 56mg; IRON 1.7mg; S 468mg; CALC 40mg

Herb-Cheese Bread

To make ahead, assemble loaf, wrap in foil, a store in refrigerator. Bring to room temperatu and bake as directed.

¼   cup reduced-calorie stick margarine
¼   cup minced green onions
2   garlic cloves, crushed
¼   teaspoon dried oregano
¼   teaspoon ground cumin
⅛   teaspoon crushed red pepper
⅛   teaspoon salt
1   (1-pound) loaf Italian bread, split
½   cup (2 ounces) shredded reduced-fat Monterey Jack cheese

Preheat oven to 400°.

Melt margarine in a small skillet over medium-
gh heat. Add green onions and garlic; sauté 2
inutes. Stir in oregano, cumin, red pepper, and
lt. Brush margarine mixture evenly over cut
les of bread. Sprinkle cheese over bottom half
loaf; top with top half of loaf. Wrap in foil, and
ke at 400° for 20 minutes. Serve warm. Yield:
servings (serving size: 1 slice).

lections: 1 FA, 1 B; **Points: 3**
r **serving:** CAL 140 (23% from fat); FAT 3.6g (sat 1g); PRO 4.9g;
RB 21.8g; FIB 1.1g; CHOL 3mg; IRON 0.9mg; SOD 313mg;
LC 48mg

ranberry-Sweet Potato
uick Bread

½ cups all-purpose flour
   cup firmly packed brown sugar
½ teaspoons baking powder
   teaspoon baking soda

½ teaspoon salt
¼ teaspoon ground cinnamon
¼ teaspoon ground nutmeg
¾ cup canned unsweetened mashed sweet
   potato
¾ cup egg substitute
⅓ cup orange juice
¼ cup margarine, melted
1 cup chopped cranberries
Cooking spray
2 tablespoons sliced almonds

1. Preheat oven to 350°.

2. Combine first 7 ingredients in a large bowl;
make a well in center of mixture. Combine sweet
potato, egg substitute, orange juice, and margarine in a bowl; add to dry ingredients, stirring
just until moist. Fold in cranberries.

3. Spoon batter into a 9- x 5-inch loaf pan coated
with cooking spray; sprinkle almonds over batter.
Bake at 350° for 1 hour and 10 minutes or until a

Teamed with a glass of milk, a slice of Cranberry-Sweet Potato Quick Bread makes a healthy breakfast-on-the-go.

Irish Wheaten Br

oden pick inserted in center comes out clean.
t cool in pan 10 minutes on a wire rack; re-
ove from pan. Let cool completely on wire rack.
ld: 16 servings (serving size: 1 slice).

ections: 1 B, 1 FA, 40 C; **Points: 3**
 serving: CAL 163 (20% from fat); FAT 3.6g (sat 0.7g); PRO
; CARB 29.3g; FIB 1.2g; CHOL 0mg; IRON 1.5mg; SOD
mg; CALC 47mg

onkey Bread

ause the dough has a tendency to drip as it bakes,
ce the Bundt pan on a baking sheet or piece of
minum foil. This prevents a mess in the oven.

(1-pound) loaves frozen white bread dough
cup sugar
cup firmly packed brown sugar
cup 1% low-fat milk
tablespoon reduced-calorie stick margarine
teaspoons ground cinnamon
cup sugar
teaspoon ground cinnamon
oking spray

Thaw dough in refrigerator for 12 hours.
Combine 1 cup sugar and next 4 ingredients in
mall saucepan; bring to a boil, and cook 1
nute. Remove sugar syrup from heat; let cool
minutes.
Preheat oven to 350°.
Cut each loaf of dough into 24 equal portions.
mbine ¼ cup sugar and ½ teaspoon cinnamon
a shallow dish; stir well. Roll each portion of
ugh in sugar mixture, and layer dough in a 12-
p Bundt pan coated with cooking spray. Pour
gar syrup over dough; cover and let rise in a
rm place (85°), free from drafts, 35 minutes or
til doubled in bulk.
Uncover, and bake at 350° for 25 minutes or
til lightly browned. Immediately loosen edges
bread from pan with a knife. Place a serving
ate, upside down, on top of pan, and invert
ead onto plate. Remove pan, and drizzle any re-
aining syrup over bread. Yield: 24 servings.

ections: 1 B, 70 C; **Points: 4**
 serving: CAL 201 (10% from fat); PRO 5.2g; FAT 2.2g (sat
g); CARB 40.1g; FIB 0g; CHOL 0mg; IRON 1.4mg; SOD 302mg;
LC 41mg

Irish Wheaten Bread

The secret to this tender bread is in your hands:
Don't overwork the dough—just lightly knead it.

2   cups all-purpose flour
2   cups whole-wheat flour
2   tablespoons sugar
1   teaspoon salt
1   teaspoon baking soda
3   tablespoons chilled stick margarine, cut
     into small pieces
1⅓ cups low-fat buttermilk
2   large egg whites
Cooking spray

1. Preheat oven to 375°.

2. Combine first 5 ingredients in a food processor; pulse until well blended. With the processor
on, drop margarine through food chute; process
10 seconds.

3. Combine buttermilk and egg whites; stir well.
With the processor on, pour mixture through
food chute; process 20 seconds or until dough
leaves sides of bowl and forms a ball. Turn dough
out onto a lightly floured surface, and lightly
knead about 10 times.

4. Pat dough into an 8-inch round cake pan
coated with cooking spray, and cut a ¼-inch-
deep X in top of dough. Bake at 375° for 45 minutes or until lightly browned. Remove bread from
pan; let cool completely on a wire rack. Cut bread
into wedges. Yield: 12 servings.

Selections: 2 B, 1 FA; **Points: 3**
Per serving: CAL 184 (17% from fat); PRO 6.3g; FAT 3.5g (sat
0.7g); CARB 32.7g; FIB 3g; CHOL 1mg; IRON 1.7mg; SOD 337mg;
CALC 46mg

BOOST THE FLAVOR

One little trick to making breads taste extra
good is to put the most flavorful ingredient
on the outside. Sprinkle seeds, herbs, or
cheese on top of muffins, loaves, rolls, or
breadsticks. It's a great way to get the flavor of higher fat ingredients such as nuts
and cheese without all the fat and calories.

Meals Made of Memories

AWAKEN ALL OF YOUR SENSES WITH
THESE MAIN DISHES.

You can thank more than your memory when a beautifully roasted chicken reminds you of those Sunday after-service meals with the family. The image of a crisp white tablecloth, plastic-covered seats, and your brother's refusal to eat anything green was brought to you courtesy of your nose. Our sense of smell, the turbobooster of taste, operates on the same nerve highway as memories and emotions. Smell is also part of a sensory dynamic duo. Taste and smell are two completely different systems, but they influence each other greatly. Lucky for us, because taste is the least sophisticated sense. That combination helps explain the power of certain foods to soothe and snuggle us in a warm blanket of memories.

But memories make poor meals. There are better ways to involve our senses with flavor. The best chefs know that taste, aroma, texture, and visual appeal are key components of flavor. By choosing an interesting dish such as roasted chicken, pasta with fresh tomato sauce, or vegetable quiche and serving it in an attractive way, you afford each of your senses an opinion in the matter.

With our easy Garlic-Rosemary Roasted Chicken you can enjoy bistro fare in your own home.

Garlic-Rosemary Roasted Chicken

The beauty of roasted chicken is its versatility. You can even serve this classic French dish with humble baked shoestring potatoes.

1 (5- to 6-pound) roasting chicken
1 tablespoon chopped fresh rosemary
8 garlic cloves, crushed
8 medium red onions
2 whole garlic heads
2 teaspoons olive oil
Rosemary sprigs (optional)

1. Preheat oven to 450°.

2. Remove giblets and neck from chicken, and discard. Rinse chicken under cold water; pat dry. Trim excess fat. Starting at neck cavity, loosen skin from breast and drumsticks by inserting fingers and gently pushing between the skin and meat. Place chopped rosemary and crushed garlic cloves beneath skin on breasts and drumsticks. Lift wing tips up and over back, and tuck under chicken.

3. Place chicken, breast side up, on a broiler pan. Cut a thin slice from end of each onion. Remove white papery skin from garlic heads (do not peel or separate the cloves). Cut tops off garlic, leaving root end intact.

4. Brush onions and garlic with olive oil. Arrange onions and garlic around chicken. Insert meat thermometer into meaty part of thigh, making sure not to touch bone. Bake at 450° for 30 minutes. Reduce oven temperature to 350°, and bake an additional 1 hour and 15 minutes or until thermometer registers 180°. Discard skin. Yield: 8 servings (serving size: 3 ounces chicken, 1 onion, and one eighth roasted garlic cloves).

Note: Spread the roasted garlic on French bread, if desired.

Selections: 3 P/M, 1 FR/V; **Points:** 5
Per serving: CAL 231 (30% from fat); FAT 7.7g (sat 1.9g); PRO 26.5g; CARB 13.5g; FIB 2.7g; CHOL 76mg; IRON 1.4mg; SOD 133mg; CALC 50mg

Baked Macaroni and Cheese

3 tablespoons reduced-calorie stick margarine
6 tablespoons all-purpose flour
¾ teaspoon dry mustard
⅛ teaspoon ground red pepper
3 cups skim milk, divided
1¼ cups (5 ounces) shredded reduced-fat sharp cheddar cheese, divided
¼ cup (1 ounce) shredded reduced-fat Swiss cheese
½ teaspoon salt
⅛ teaspoon black pepper
5 cups cooked large elbow macaroni (about 2 cups uncooked)

1. Preheat oven to 350°.

The irresistible creaminess of macaroni and cheese makes it a universal favorite.

2. Melt margarine in a large saucepan over medium heat. Stir in flour, mustard, and red pepper. Gradually add 1 cup milk, stirring with a whisk until smooth. Cook 1 minute, stirring constantly. Gradually stir in remaining 2 cups milk; cook 10 minutes or until slightly thick and bubbly, stirring constantly. Remove from heat; add ¾ cup cheddar cheese, Swiss cheese, salt, and pepper, stirring until cheese melts. Stir in macaroni.

3. Divide mixture evenly among 6 (8-ounce) ramekins; sprinkle evenly with remaining ½ cup cheddar cheese. Cover and bake at 350° for 30 minutes. Let stand, covered, 5 minutes before serving. Yield: 6 servings.

Note: Spoon macaroni mixture into a 2-quart casserole, if desired, and bake as directed.

Selections: 1 FA, 2 B, 2 P/M; **Points:** 7
Per serving: CAL 346 (26% from fat); PRO 18.9g; FAT 10.1g (sat 3.9g); CARB 44.7g; FIB 2g; CHOL 21mg; IRON 2.1mg; SOD 494mg; CALC 425mg

Cornish Hens With Rosemary-Wine Sauce

2 (1-pound) Cornish hens
Cooking spray
1 cup dry white wine
⅓ cup white wine vinegar

Baked Macaroni and Cheese

2 tablespoons low-sodium soy sauce
1 teaspoon dried rosemary, crushed
¼ teaspoon dried thyme
4 garlic cloves, minced

1. Preheat oven to 350°.

2. Remove and discard giblets from hens. Rinse hens under cold water, and pat dry. Remove skin, and trim excess fat; split hens in half lengthwise. Place hen halves, meaty sides up, in a 13- x 9-inch baking dish coated with cooking spray.

3. Combine wine and next 5 ingredients, and pour over hens. Bake at 350° for 1 hour or until done, basting occasionally with wine mixture. Yield: 4 servings.

Selections: 3 P/M; **Points:** 4
Per serving: CAL 185 (33% from fat); PRO 26.2g; FAT 6.8g (sat 1.8g); CARB 2g; FIB 0.1g; CHOL 80mg; IRON 1.6mg; SOD 279mg; CALC 29mg

Beer-Batter Baked Fish

1 tablespoon all-purpose flour
¼ teaspoon salt
4 (6-ounce) orange roughy or other lean white fish fillets
Cooking spray
½ cup all-purpose flour
¼ teaspoon pepper
½ cup beer
1 tablespoon extra-virgin olive oil
1 large egg yolk
2 large egg whites (at room temperature)

1. Preheat oven to 500°.

2. Sprinkle 1 tablespoon flour and salt over 1 side of fillets. Place fillets, flour sides up, in a 13- x 9-inch baking dish coated with cooking spray.

3. Combine ½ cup flour and pepper in a medium bowl. Gradually add beer, oil, and egg yolk, stirring with a whisk until blended.

4. Beat egg whites at high speed of a mixer until stiff peaks form. Gently fold egg whites into beer mixture, and spread evenly over fillets. Bake at 500° for 10 minutes. Yield: 4 servings.

Selections: 2 P/M, 1 B, 1 FA; **Points:** 5
Per serving: CAL 248 (22% from fat); PRO 29.3g; FAT 6.2g (sat 0.9g); CARB 14.7g; FIB 0.5g; CHOL 88mg; IRON 1.3mg; SOD 430mg; CALC 13mg

Pecan Catfish

ecan Catfish

(4-ounce) farm-raised catfish fillets
cup fresh whole-wheat breadcrumbs
ooking spray
cup fat-free sour cream
tablespoon lemon juice
tablespoon Dijon mustard
tablespoons chopped pecans, toasted

Preheat oven to 500°.

Dredge fillets in breadcrumbs, and place fillets
broiler pan coated with cooking spray. Bake at
00° for 10 minutes or until fish flakes easily
hen tested with a fork. Arrange fillets on a serv-
g platter; set aside, and keep warm.

Combine sour cream, lemon juice, and mus-
rd in a saucepan; cook over medium-low heat
til warm (do not boil), stirring constantly.
oon sauce over fillets; sprinkle with pecans.
eld: 6 servings (serving size: 1 fillet, 1 table-
oon sauce, and 1½ teaspoons pecans).

lections: 1 P/M, 1 FA, 40 C; **Points:** 4
r serving: CAL 190 (37% from fat); PRO 22.6g; FAT 7.8g (sat
g); CARB 6.2g; FIB 0.6g; CHOL 66mg; IRON 1.4mg; SOD
2mg; CALC 76mg

emon-Broiled Orange Roughy

(4-ounce) orange roughy fillets
ooking spray
tablespoons lemon juice
tablespoon Dijon mustard
tablespoon reduced-calorie stick
margarine, melted
teaspoon coarsely ground pepper
dditional coarsely ground pepper (optional)

Place fillets on broiler pan coated with cooking
ray. Combine lemon juice and next 3 ingredi-
ts; stir well. Drizzle half of juice mixture over
lets. Broil 8 minutes or until fish flakes easily
hen tested with a fork.

Place fillets on a plate, and drizzle remaining
ice mixture over fillets. Sprinkle with additional
pper, if desired. Yield: 4 servings.

lections: 1 P/M, 1 FA; **Points:** 5
r serving: CAL 204 (56% from fat); PRO 20g; FAT 12.6g (sat
g); CARB 1.3g; FIB 0g; CHOL 54mg; IRON 0.6mg; SOD 204mg;
LC 36mg

Farmhouse Strata

8   ounces turkey Italian sausage
2   cups egg substitute
1   cup skim milk
½   cup (2 ounces) shredded reduced-fat
    cheddar cheese
½   teaspoon dry mustard
¼   teaspoon rubbed sage
Dash of salt
Dash of ground red pepper
¼   cup chopped green onions
6   (1-ounce) slices white bread, cut into
    ½-inch cubes
Cooking spray
2   medium tomatoes, cut into ¼-inch-thick
    slices

1. Remove casings from sausage. Cook sausage in
a nonstick skillet over medium-high heat until
browned, stirring to crumble. Drain well.

2. Combine egg substitute and next 6 ingredients in a bowl; stir well with a whisk. Add
sausage, green onions, and bread cubes, and stir
well. Pour mixture into an 11- x 7-inch baking
dish coated with cooking spray. Cover and chill
at least 8 hours.

3. Preheat oven to 350°.

4. Bake, uncovered, at 350° for 45 minutes or until
set and lightly browned. Cut into squares; top each
serving with tomato slices. Yield: 6 servings.

Selections: 3 P/M, 1 B; **Points:** 5
Per serving: CAL 246 (33% from fat); PRO 19.5g; FAT 9.0g (sat
3.6g); CARB 21.1g; FIB 1.5g; CHOL 24mg; IRON 3mg; SOD
603mg; CALC 206mg

Pick the Perfect Fish

*Knowing what to look for when buying fish
takes practice. Our hints will get you started.*

• **Whole fish:** bright, bulging eyes; fiery red
gills; shiny skin; mild odor.

• **Fillets or steaks:** firm, shiny flesh with no
tears or signs of discoloration; mild odor.

• **In general:** If you're not satisfied with the fish
in your supermarket's seafood case, ask to buy
some that is still frozen. Frozen seafood that is
thawed at home (in the refrigerator or under
cold running water) will often taste fresher.

Ham-and-Cheese-Stuffed Potatoes

4   (12-ounce) baking potatoes
2   tablespoons reduced-calorie stick margarine
2   cups broccoli florets
½   cup chopped onion
½   cup low-salt chicken broth
1   cup diced lean, lower-salt ham
¼   teaspoon freshly ground pepper
6   tablespoons fat-free sour cream, divided
Cooking spray
½   cup (2 ounces) shredded reduced-fat cheddar cheese

1. Preheat oven to 400°.

2. Bake potatoes at 400° for 1 hour and 15 minutes or until tender. Let cool slightly.

3. Melt margarine in a nonstick skillet over medium-high heat. Add broccoli and onion; sauté 3 minutes. Add broth; bring to a boil. Cover, reduce heat, and simmer 5 minutes or until broccoli is tender. Remove from heat; stir in ham and pepper.

4. Cut a lengthwise strip from top of each potato; discard strips. Scoop out pulp, leaving ¼-inch-thick shells; set shells aside.

5. Place potato pulp in a bowl; add 2 tablespoons sour cream, and mash to desired consistency. Stir in broccoli mixture. Spoon mixture evenly into potato shells.

Packed with vegetables and protein, Ham-and-Cheese-Stuffed Potatoes makes a complete meal.

6. Place potatoes in an 11- x 7-inch baking di[sh] coated with cooking spray. Bake at 400° for [#] minutes or until thoroughly heated. Top ea[ch] potato with 2 tablespoons cheese, and bake [an] additional 3 minutes or until cheese melts. T[op] each potato with 1 tablespoon sour crea[m]. Yield: 4 servings.

Selections: 2 B, 1 FA, 1 FR/V, 3 P/M; **Points:** 7
Per serving: CAL 385 (21% from fat); PRO 20.6 g; FAT 8.9g ([SAT] 2.8g); CARB 58.3g; FIB 6.5g; CHOL 26mg; IRON 4.6mg; SOD 4[##] mg; CALC 215.8mg

Chicken Club

2   tablespoons no-salt-added tomato juice
2   tablespoons balsamic vinegar
2   (4-ounce) skinned, boned chicken breast halves
Cooking spray
Dash of pepper
1   tablespoon light mayonnaise
6   (¾-ounce) slices reduced-calorie sourdough bread, toasted
2   cups torn romaine lettuce
8   (¼-inch-thick) slices tomato (about 1 medium)
4   turkey-bacon slices, cooked and cut in ha[lf] crosswise

1. Combine tomato juice and vinegar in a sha[l]low dish; set aside.

2. Place each piece of chicken between 2 shee[ts] of heavy-duty plastic wrap, and flatten to ¼-inch thickness using a meat mallet or rolli[ng] pin. Add chicken to vinegar mixture. Cover an[d] marinate in refrigerator at least 1 hour, turnin[g] chicken occasionally.

3. Remove chicken from marinade; discard mar[i]nade. Coat a large nonstick skillet with cooki[ng] spray, and place over medium heat until hot. Ad[d] chicken; cook 2 minutes on each side or unt[il] done. Remove from skillet, and sprinkle wi[th] pepper; set aside, and keep warm.

4. Spread half of mayonnaise over 2 bread slic[es]. Top each bread slice with ½ cup lettuce, [#] tomato slices, and 1 chicken breast half; cov[er] with another slice of bread. Top bread with [½] cup lettuce, 2 tomato slices, and 4 half-slices [of]

...con. Spread remaining half of mayonnaise over [re]maining 2 bread slices; place on top of each [san]dwich. Cut each sandwich in half, and secure [wit]h wooden picks. Yield: 2 servings.

[Sel]ections: 3 P/M, 2 B, 1 FA, 2 FR/V, 60 C; **Points:** 7
[Per] serving: CAL 370 (26% from fat); PRO 38.9g; FAT 10.5g (SAT [?]g); CARB 32.9g; FIB 7.9g; CHOL 94.5mg; IRON 1.8mg; SOD [?]mg; CALC 37mg

[Ro]asted Vegetable Pitas With [So]ur Cream Dressing

[Fo]r this sandwich, feel free to experiment with other [veg]etables. Eggplant, yellow squash, and red bell [pe]pper work well.

[2] tablespoons (½ ounce) crumbled feta
 cheese
[2] tablespoons fat-free sour cream
[2] tablespoons skim milk
[1] teaspoon prepared horseradish
[Da]sh of pepper
[2] cup sliced zucchini
[1] large tomato (about 8 ounces), cut into 8
 wedges

1   cup (1-inch) pieces green bell pepper
1   medium onion (about 8 ounces), cut into
    8 wedges
½   teaspoon dried oregano
1½ teaspoons olive oil
¼   teaspoon salt
2   garlic cloves, minced
Cooking spray
1   (7-inch) pita bread round, cut in half

1. Combine first 5 ingredients in a small bowl; stir well, and set aside.

2. Combine zucchini and next 7 ingredients in a bowl; toss gently. Spoon vegetable mixture onto a broiler pan coated with cooking spray. Broil 10 minutes or until tender and lightly browned, stirring occasionally.

3. Divide vegetable mixture evenly between pita halves. Drizzle 2 tablespoons dressing over each sandwich. Yield: 2 servings.

Selections: 2 FR/V, 1 FA, 1 B; **Points:** 4
Per serving: CAL 208 (30% from fat); PRO 7.7g; FAT 6.9g (sat 1.9g); CARB 30.8g; FIB 4.2g; CHOL 7mg; IRON 2.4mg; SOD 532mg; CALC 115mg

Our Chicken Club is just as hearty and satisfying as the one served at the local grill but without the guilt.

Penne With Chunky Tomato Sauce

enne With Chunky Tomato
auce

live oil-flavored cooking spray
  teaspoon olive oil
  cup finely chopped onion
  garlic clove, minced
  (14½-ounce) cans no-salt-added whole
    tomatoes, undrained and chopped
  cup no-salt-added tomato sauce
  teaspoon salt
  teaspoon freshly ground pepper
  cups hot cooked penne (about 16 ounces
    uncooked short tubular pasta)
  cup thinly sliced fresh basil
  tablespoons (¾ ounce) grated fresh
    Parmesan cheese
sil sprigs (optional)

Coat a large nonstick skillet with
oking spray; add oil, and place
er medium heat until hot. Add
ion and garlic; sauté until tender.
d tomatoes and tomato sauce;
ing to a boil. Reduce heat, and
nmer, uncovered, 20 minutes or
til thick, stirring occasionally. Stir
salt and pepper.

Combine tomato mixture and pasta in a bowl;
ss gently to coat. Sprinkle with sliced basil and
eese. Garnish with basil sprigs, if desired. Yield:
servings (serving size: 1½ cups).

lections: 1 FR/V, 4 B; **Points:** 6
r serving: CAL 337 (7% from fat); PRO 12.1g; FAT 2.7g (sat
g); CARB 65.9g; FIB 3.4g; CHOL 2mg; IRON 3.7mg; SOD
4mg; CALC 97mg

alian Meatball Sandwich

  (2-ounce) whole-wheat submarine rolls
  pound ground round
  cup finely chopped onion
  tablespoons Italian-seasoned breadcrumbs
  tablespoons water
  teaspoon pepper
  large egg white, lightly beaten
oking spray
½ cups low-fat, reduced-sodium pasta sauce
  cup (3 ounces) shredded part-skim
    mozzarella cheese
sil sprigs (optional)

1. Cut an oval piece out of top of each roll; set rolls aside, reserving top pieces for another use.

2. Combine beef and next 5 ingredients in a bowl; stir well. Shape mixture into 36 (1-inch) balls.

3. Preheat oven to 400°.

4. Coat a large nonstick skillet with cooking spray; place over medium heat until hot. Add meatballs, and cook 8 minutes, browning on all sides. Drain meatballs in a colander. Wipe drippings from skillet with a paper towel.

5. Return meatballs to skillet; add pasta sauce, and cook over medium-low heat 10 minutes or until thoroughly heated. Set aside, and keep warm.

6. Place submarine rolls on a baking sheet; fill each with 6 meatballs. Spoon sauce evenly over meatballs; sprinkle evenly with cheese. Bake at 400° for 5 minutes or until cheese melts. Garnish with basil sprigs, if desired. Yield: 6 servings.

Selections: 2 P/M, 2 B, 1 FR/V; **Points:** 6
Per serving: CAL 269 (25% from fat); PRO 25.8g; FAT 7.6g (sat 2.4g); CARB 23.4g; FIB 1.2; CHOL 60mg; IRON 1.7mg; SOD 621mg; CALC 100mg

No dish embodies simplicity and goodness like pasta with vegetables.

Spaghetti Carbonara

1   tablespoon all-purpose flour
1   cup evaporated skim milk
¼   cup egg substitute
2   tablespoons chopped fresh parsley
1   teaspoon chopped fresh basil
1   garlic clove, minced
4   cups hot cooked spaghetti (about 8 ounces
      uncooked pasta)
1   cup frozen green peas and carrots, thawed
¼   cup (1 ounce) grated fresh Parmesan
      cheese
4   turkey-bacon slices, cooked and crumbled
½   teaspoon freshly ground pepper

1. Place flour in a medium saucepan. Gradually add milk, stirring with a whisk until blended. Place over medium heat; cook until mixture is slightly thick, stirring constantly. Gradually stir about one-fourth of hot milk mixture into egg substitute. Add to remaining milk mixture; cook

MEAT: PART OF A HEALTHY DIET

Meat doesn't have to be the villain. It's rich in protein, iron, zinc, and B vitamins and, when wisely used, can be a valuable part of a low-fat, healthy diet. Here are some pointers for finding the leanest cuts.

• Cuts of beef with the words "loin" (sirloin, tenderloin) and "round" (eye-of-round, top round) have the least amount of fat.

• The leanest cuts of pork and lamb come from the "loin" and the "leg."

• All veal cuts are low in fat; however, veal is higher in cholesterol than other lean cuts of meat.

• For ground meat, choose ground chuck, or preferably ground round, or ultra-lean ground beef.

• In whole cuts, look for the cut with the least marbling, or white veins of fat, in it.

• If the beef carries a grade, look for "Select" and "Choice."

until thick, stirring constantly. Remove from heat; stir in parsley, basil, and garlic.

2. Combine sauce and pasta in a large bowl; toss gently to coat. Add remaining ingredients; toss gently. Yield: 4 servings (serving size: 1½ cups).

Selections: 3 B, 1 P/M, 50 C; Points: 7
Per serving: CAL 358 (13% from fat); PRO 19.8g; FAT 2.3g (sat 0.2g); CARB 44.7g; FIB 2.6g; CHOL 25mg; IRON 3.4mg; SOD 650mg; CALC 314mg

Summertime Roast Beef Subs

1¼ cups fresh corn kernels or frozen whole-kernel corn, thawed
⅓ cup diced red bell pepper
¼ cup diced red onion
¼ cup light Caesar dressing
4 (3-ounce) submarine rolls
4 red leaf lettuce leaves
8 (¼-inch-thick) slices tomato
8 (1-ounce) slices lean cooked roast beef

1. Combine first 4 ingredients in a bowl; stir well, and set aside.

2. Cut a ¼-inch-thick slice off top of each roll; set tops aside. Hollow out centers of rolls, leaving ½-inch-thick shells; reserve torn bread for another use. Place 1 lettuce leaf in bottom half of each roll. Spoon corn mixture evenly over lettuce; top each serving with 2 slices tomato and 2 slices roast beef. Cover with roll tops. Yield: 4 servings.

Selections: 4 B, 1 FR/V, 2 P/M; Points: 9
Per serving: CAL 427g (27% from fat); PRO 24.2g; FAT 12.9g (sat 2.6g); CARB 53.5g; FIB 2.8g; CHOL 62mg; IRON 3.3mg; SOD 534mg; CALC 53mg

Smothered Steak and Onions

1 teaspoon beef-flavored bouillon granules
1 cup hot water
4 (4-ounce) cubed sirloin steaks
½ teaspoon salt-free lemon-herb seasoning
Cooking spray
1 medium onion, sliced and separated into rings
1 tablespoon cornstarch
¼ cup water
2 cups hot cooked long-grain rice
Parsley sprigs (optional)

1. Combine bouillon granules and hot water; stir well, and set aside. Sprinkle steaks with lemon-

herb seasoning. Coat a large nonstick skillet wi cooking spray; place over medium heat until ho Add steaks; cook 2 minutes on each side or un browned. Add onion and bouillon; bring to boil. Cover, reduce heat, and simmer 12 minut or until onion is tender. Remove steaks and onio from skillet with a slotted spoon; set aside, a keep warm.

2. Combine cornstarch and ¼ cup water; st well. Add to cooking liquid in skillet; cook ov medium heat until thick and bubbly, stirrir constantly. Place rice on plates, and top wi steak and onion. Divide gravy evenly over eac serving. Garnish with parsley sprigs, if desire Yield: 4 servings.

Selections: 3 P/M, 1 B; Points: 6
Per serving: CAL 305 (19% from fat); PRO 27.1g; FAT 6.4g (s 2.2g); CARB 32g; FIB 1.1g; CHOL 69mg; IRON 4.4mg; SO 31.7mg; CALC 25mg

Peppercorn-Crusted Pork Loin Roast

1 (2½-pound) lean boned pork loin roast
3 tablespoons Dijon mustard
1 tablespoon low-fat buttermilk
2 cups fresh whole-wheat breadcrumbs
2 tablespoons cracked pepper
2 teaspoons mixed peppercorns, crushed
2 teaspoons chopped fresh thyme
¼ teaspoon salt
Cooking spray
Creamy Peppercorn Sauce
Thyme sprigs (optional)

1. Preheat oven to 325°.

2. Trim fat from roast. Combine mustard an buttermilk. Spread mustard mixture over roas

3. Combine breadcrumbs, pepper, peppercorn thyme, and salt in a bowl; press breadcrum mixture evenly onto roast. Place roast on broiler pan coated with cooking spray. Inse meat thermometer into thickest part of roas Bake at 325° for 2 hours or until meat the mometer registers 160°(pork will be slight pink in center). Let roast stand 10 minutes be fore slicing. Serve with Creamy Peppercor

...auce. Garnish with thyme sprigs, if desired. ...ield: 10 servings (serving size: 3 ounces pork ...nd 2 tablespoons sauce).

...reamy Peppercorn Sauce:

- cup low-fat buttermilk
- cup fat-free sour cream
- tablespoons grated Parmesan cheese
- tablespoons light mayonnaise
- ...₂ tablespoons lemon juice
- ...₂ teaspoons mixed peppercorns, crushed
- teaspoon salt

...Combine all ingredients in a small bowl; stir ...ll. Yield: 1¼ cups.

...lections: 3 P/M, 50 C; **Points:** 5.5
... **serving:** CAL 241 (38% from fat); PRO 26.7g; FAT 10.1g (sat ...g); CARB 10g; FIB 0.8g; CHOL 70mg; IRON 2.9mg; SOD ...mg; CALC 80mg

...erbed Pot Roast

- (4½-pound) lean, boned rump roast
- cup dry red wine
- cup no-salt-added tomato sauce

¼ cup white vinegar
1 tablespoon spicy hot mustard
1 teaspoon dried thyme
¼ teaspoon dried oregano
¼ teaspoon ground red pepper
2 shallots, minced
1 bay leaf

1. Trim fat from roast. Combine roast and remaining ingredients in a large heavy-duty zip-top plastic bag. Seal bag, and marinate in refrigerator 8 hours, turning bag occasionally.

2. Preheat oven to 350°.

3. Place roast and marinade in a large ovenproof Dutch oven. Cover and bake at 350° for 2½ hours or until tender.

4. Remove roast from pan; discard cooking liquid. Place roast on a serving platter; let stand 10 minutes before slicing. Yield: 15 servings (serving size: 3 ounces).

Selections: 3 P/M; **Points:** 4
Per serving: CAL 188 (26% from fat); PRO 31.2g; FAT 5.5g (sat 2.0g); CARB 1.2g; FIB 0g; CHOL 78mg; IRON 3mg; SOD 83mg; CALC 6mg

This colorful Peppercorn-Crusted Pork Loin Roast makes a nice presentation for dinner guests.

The simple topping of lemon-garlic breadcrumbs perfectly complements the shrimp in Garlicky Baked Shrimp.

Garlicky Baked Shrimp

Cooking spray
1¼ pounds medium shrimp, peeled and
    deveined
½ cup dry breadcrumbs
3 tablespoons finely chopped fresh parsley
1 teaspoon grated lemon rind
¼ teaspoon salt
3 garlic cloves, minced
2 tablespoons fresh lemon juice
4 teaspoons olive oil

1. Preheat oven to 400°.

2. Coat 4 individual gratin dishes with cooking spray. Divide shrimp among dishes; set aside.

3. Combine breadcrumbs and next 4 ingredients; stir in juice and oil. Sprinkle breadcrumb mixture over shrimp. Place dishes on a baking sheet. Bake at 400° for 13 minutes or until shrimp are done and breadcrumbs are lightly browned. Yield: 4 servings.

Selections: 2 P/M, 1 B, 1 FA; **Points:** 5
Per serving: CAL 220 (30% from fat); PRO 24.7g; FAT 7.3g (s 1.1g); CARB 12.5g; FIB 0.7g; CHOL 170mg; IRON 3.8mg; SC 431mg; CALC 99mg

Chicken and Dumplings

6½ cups water, divided
4 (4-ounce) skinned, boned chicken breast
    halves
1½ cups sliced mushrooms
¾ cup diced carrot
2 tablespoons chopped onion
1 teaspoon lemon juice
¾ teaspoon poultry seasoning
¼ teaspoon salt
¼ teaspoon pepper
4 drops hot sauce
1 garlic clove, minced
1⅓ cups all-purpose flour, divided
1 teaspoon baking powder
½ cup skim milk

. Combine 6 cups water and next 4 ingredients 1 a large Dutch oven; bring to a boil. Cover, reduce heat, and simmer 30 minutes or until hicken is tender. Remove chicken with a slotted poon, and cut into bite-size pieces. Return hicken to pan; cover and chill 8 hours.

. Skim fat from chicken mixture, and discard. Bring chicken mixture to a boil over medium heat, tirring occasionally. Stir in lemon juice, poultry easoning, salt, pepper, hot sauce, and garlic.

. Place 1/3 cup flour in a bowl. Gradually add remaining 1/2 cup water, stirring well with whisk. Add to chicken mixture, stirring constantly. Reduce heat, and simmer, uncovered, 35 minutes, tirring occasionally.

. Combine remaining 1 cup flour and baking owder in a bowl; stir well. Add milk, stirring just ntil dry ingredients are moist. Drop batter by evel teaspoons into simmering chicken mixture; over, reduce heat, and simmer 14 minutes or unil dumplings are done. Yield: 6 servings.

elections: 2 P/M, 1 B; Points: 5
er serving: CAL 233 (15% from fat); PRO 23.1g; FAT 4g (sat .7g); CARB 23.5g; FIB 1.3g; CHOL 49mg; IRON 2.3mg; SOD 19mg; CALC 91mg

Creamy Chicken-and-Rice Casserole

(6.9-ounce) package one-third-less-salt chicken-flavored rice-and-vermicelli mix with chicken broth and herbs
tablespoon margarine
2¼ cups hot water
Cooking spray
1½ pounds skinned, boned chicken breasts, cut into bite-size pieces
cup presliced fresh mushrooms
½ teaspoon garlic powder
¼ cup fat-free sour cream
¼ teaspoon pepper
(10¾-ounce) can condensed reduced-fat reduced-sodium cream of mushroom soup, undiluted
¼ cup crushed multigrain crackers (about 6 crackers)
tablespoon margarine, melted
½ teaspoon poppy seeds

1. Cook rice mix in a nonstick skillet according to package directions, using 1 tablespoon margarine and 2¼ cups hot water. Remove mixture from skillet; set aside. Wipe skillet with a paper towel.

2. Preheat oven to 350°.

3. Coat skillet with cooking spray, and place over high heat until hot. Add chicken, mushrooms, and garlic powder, and sauté 6 minutes or until chicken loses its pink color. Combine chicken mixture, rice mixture, sour cream, pepper, and soup in a bowl, and stir well. Spoon mixture into a 2-quart casserole coated with cooking spray. Combine cracker crumbs, melted margarine, and poppy seeds; stir well. Sprinkle cracker-crumb mixture over chicken mixture. Bake at 350° for 35 minutes or until thoroughly heated. Yield: 6 servings (serving size: 1⅓ cups).

Make-Ahead Tip: You can assemble the casserole ahead of time, omitting the cracker-crumb mixture; cover and chill in the refrigerator or freeze (thaw frozen casserole overnight in refrigerator). Let stand at room temperature 30 minutes; top with cracker-crumb mixture, and bake as directed.

Selections: 1 B, 1 FA, 3 P/M, 80 C; **Points:** 7
Per serving: CAL 334 (18% from fat); PRO 32.2g; FAT 6.8g (sat 1.6g); CARB 30g; FIB 0.2g; CHOL 68mg; IRON 2mg; SOD 687mg; CALC 19mg

Chicken Salad in Cantaloupe

3 cups shredded cooked chicken breast
1½ cups cubed peeled papaya
1 cup finely chopped red bell pepper
¼ cup minced fresh cilantro
3 tablespoons white balsamic vinegar
1½ tablespoons lime juice
1½ tablespoons Dijon mustard
4 teaspoons honey
2 teaspoons olive oil
¼ teaspoon ground red pepper
2 small cantaloupes
Lime wedges (optional)

1. Combine first 4 ingredients; toss gently. Combine vinegar and next 5 ingredients; stir well. Pour over chicken mixture; toss gently. Cover and chill.

2. Cut each cantaloupe in half; discard seeds. Cut

a thin slice from bottom of each melon half so it will sit flat, if necessary. Spoon chicken mixture evenly into melon halves. Garnish with lime wedges, if desired. Yield: 4 servings.

Selections: 3 P/M, 3 FR/V, 1 FA; **Points:** 7
Per serving: CAL 366 (19% from fat); PRO 38.4g; FAT 7.7g (sat 1.9g); CARB 37.5g; FIB 5g; CHOL 96mg; IRON 2.7mg; SOD 281mg; CALC 70mg

Vegetable-Gruyere Quiche

1   cup julienne-cut leek
2   cups julienne-cut zucchini
2   cups julienne-cut yellow squash
1   cup julienne-cut red bell pepper
1⅓ cups all-purpose flour
¼   cup margarine
2 to 3 tablespoons ice water
Cooking spray
2   large eggs
1   large egg white
2   tablespoons 1% low-fat milk
1   teaspoon dried Italian seasoning
½   teaspoon salt
¼   teaspoon pepper
¼   cup (1 ounce) finely shredded reduced-fat Gruyere cheese

1. Add water to a Dutch oven to a depth of 2 inches; bring to a boil. Add leek; cover and simmer 5 minutes. Add zucchini, squash, and bell pepper; cover and simmer 5 minutes. Drain well; pat vegetables dry with paper towels.

2. Place flour in a bowl; cut in margarine with a pastry blender or 2 knives until mixture resembles coarse meal. Sprinkle ice water, 1 tablespoon at a time, evenly over surface of mixture; toss with a fork until moist.

3. Press mixture gently into a 4-inch circle on heavy-duty plastic wrap, and cover with additional plastic wrap. Chill 20 minutes. Roll dough, still covered, to a 12-inch circle. Place dough in freezer 5 minutes or until plastic wrap can be easily removed.

4. Preheat oven to 450°.

5. Remove 1 sheet of plastic wrap; fit dough into a 9-inch quiche dish or pie plate coated with cooking spray. Remove top sheet of plastic wrap.

Fold edges of pastry under and flute. Bake at 450° for 5 minutes. Reduce oven temperature to 375°.

6. Spoon vegetable mixture into pastry. Combine eggs, egg white, and next 4 ingredients in a bowl; stir well with a whisk. Pour egg mixture into pastry. Bake at 375° for 30 minutes; sprinkle with cheese. Bake an additional 5 minutes or until cheese melts. Let stand 5 minutes before serving. Yield: 4 servings.

Selections: 1 FR/V, 2 B, 3 FA, 1 P/M; **Points:** 8
Per serving: CAL 384 (38% from fat); PRO 14g; FAT 16.3g (sat 4.0g); CARB 46.8g; FIB 4.1g; CHOL 115mg; IRON 4.7mg; SOD 501mg; CALC 181mg

Denver Omelets

2   teaspoons reduced-calorie stick margarine, divided
1   cup chopped onion
½   cup coarsely chopped red bell pepper
½   cup coarsely chopped green bell pepper
⅓   cup diced lean lower-salt ham
2   large eggs
4   large egg whites
¼   teaspoon salt

1. Melt 1 teaspoon margarine in a small nonstick skillet over medium-high heat. Add onion and bell peppers; sauté 7 minutes or until tender. Add ham; sauté 1 minute. Remove mixture from skillet; set aside.

2. Combine eggs, egg whites, and salt in a medium bowl; stir well with a whisk.

3. Melt ½ teaspoon margarine in skillet over medium heat. Spread ½ cup onion mixture over bottom of skillet. Pour half of egg mixture into skillet; top with ½ cup onion mixture (do not stir). Cover, reduce heat to medium-low, and cook 10 minutes or until center is set. Loosen omelet with a spatula, and fold in half. Slide omelet onto an individual plate; set aside, and keep warm. Repeat procedure with remaining ½ teaspoon margarine, onion mixture, and egg mixture. Yield: 2 servings (serving size: 1 omelet)

Selections: 1 FA, 1 FR/V, 3 P/M; **Points:** 4.5
Per serving: CAL 215 (40% from fat); PRO 20g; FAT 9.5g (sat 2.5g); CARB 13.2g; FIB 2.8g; CHOL 235mg; IRON 1.9mg; SOD 724mg; CALC 53mg

LEEKS: A WELL-KEPT SECRET

Leeks, which look like large green onions, have a unique sweet onion flavor that makes them a delicious vegetable side dish. When you plan to use leeks, keep these tips in mind:

• When shopping for leeks, look for crisp green tops, and choose the bundle with the longest white stems. This is the usable part of the vegetable.

• Leeks that are larger than 1½ inches in diameter tend to have a stronger flavor and may be a little tough.

• Store unwashed leeks up to five days in a zip-top plastic bag in the vegetable bin of the refrigerator.

• Even clean-looking leeks may hide sand and dirt between their leaves. Clean them thoroughly by pulling the leaves apart under cold running water.

Serve Bourbon-Bacon
Scallops over rice with
a side of snow peas
and broccoli.

Bourbon-Bacon Scallops

For best flavor, use pure maple syrup rather than pancake syrup or artificially flavored syrup.

3   tablespoons minced green onions
2   tablespoons bourbon
2   tablespoons maple syrup
1   tablespoon low-sodium soy sauce
1   tablespoon Dijon mustard
¼   teaspoon pepper
24 large sea scallops (about 1½ pounds)
6   low-sodium bacon slices (4 ounces)
Cooking spray

1. Combine first 6 ingredients in a large bowl, and stir well. Add scallops, stirring gently to coat. Cover and marinate in refrigerator 1 hour, stirring occasionally.

2. Remove scallops from bowl, reserving marinade. Cut each slice of bacon into 4 pieces. Wrap 1 bacon piece around each scallop (bacon might only wrap halfway around scallops if they are very large). Thread scallops onto 4 (12-inch) skewers, leaving some space between scallops so bacon will cook.

3. Place skewers on a broiler pan coated with cooking spray; broil 8 minutes or until bacon crisp and scallops are done, basting occasional with reserved marinade (cooking time will va greatly with size of scallops). Yield: 4 servin (serving size: 6 scallops).

Selections: 2 P/M, 90 C; **Points:** 5.5
Per serving: CAL 245 (26% from fat); FAT 7g (sat 2g); PRO 32.4 CARB 11.3g; FIB 0.1g; CHOL 68mg; IRON 0.7mg; SOD 642m CALC 51mg

Grilled Mint-Lamb Chops

8   (4-ounce) lean lamb loin chops (about 1
    inch thick)
½   cup grated fresh onion
6   tablespoons chopped fresh mint, divided
½   teaspoon pepper
1   large garlic clove, crushed
Cooking spray

1. Trim fat from chops. Combine onion, 4 tabl spoons mint, pepper, and garlic in a large heav duty zip-top plastic bag. Add chops; seal bag, an marinate in refrigerator at least 3 hours.

2. Remove chops from bag; discard marinad Prepare grill. Place chops on grill rack coate th cooking spray; grill, covered, 5 minutes on ch side or until desired degree of doneness.

Place chops on plates; sprinkle with remaining tablespoons mint. Yield: 4 servings (serving e: 2 chops and 1½ teaspoons mint).

Selections: 3 P/M; **Points:** 5.5
r serving: CAL 238 (40% from fat); PRO 32.1g; FAT 10.5g (sat g); CARB 1.5g; FIB 0.3g; CHOL 101mg; IRON 2.2mg; SOD mg; CALC 26mg

lama's Meat Loaf

rve leftover meat loaf slices on whole-wheat bread ith mayonnaise, lettuce, and cheddar cheese.

cup chopped onion
cup chopped green bell pepper
tablespoons minced fresh parsley
teaspoon pepper
teaspoon salt
garlic cloves, minced
large egg, lightly beaten
(1-ounce) slice white bread, torn into
small pieces
½ pounds ground round
ooking spray
cup ketchup

Preheat oven to 350°.

Combine first 8 ingredients in a large bowl, ssing until bread pieces are moist. Crumble ef over onion mixture, and stir just until ended. Pack mixture into a 9- x 5-inch loaf n coated with cooking spray. Spread ketchup

over top of loaf. Bake at 350° for 1 hour or until meat loaf registers 160°. Let loaf stand in pan 10 minutes.

3. Remove meat loaf from pan; cut loaf into 6 slices. Yield: 6 servings (serving size: 1 slice).

Selections: 3 P/M, 50 C; **Points:** 5
Per serving: CAL 220 (28% from fat); PRO 27.4g; FAT 6.9g (sat 2.4g); CARB 10.8g; FIB 1.4g; CHOL 101mg; IRON 3.4mg; SOD 552mg; CALC 29mg

Ham Steak With Pineapple Sauce

Serve with sweet potato wedges, steamed zucchini, and corn muffins to complement this pineapple-fla-vored sauce.

1 (1-pound) slice 33%-less-sodium cooked ham (about ½ inch thick)
1 tablespoon lemon juice
2 teaspoons brown sugar
1 teaspoon Dijon mustard
⅛ teaspoon ground ginger
½ cup pineapple juice
1 teaspoon cornstarch

1. Trim fat from ham. Lightly score ham slice in a diamond pattern using a sharp knife. Place in an 11- x 7-inch baking dish. Combine next 4 ingredients in a bowl, stirring well with a whisk; spread mixture over ham. Cover with heavy-duty plastic wrap, and vent. Microwave at HIGH 4 minutes or until thoroughly heated. Remove ham from

Mama's Meat Loaf, mashed potatoes, and green peas will soothe your soul.

CHOLESTEROL-EGG DEBATE

New research reveals that dietary cholesterol affects people's blood cholesterol levels differently. Some people can compensate for an increase in dietary cholesterol, while others cannot.

Although knowing your body's response to dietary cholesterol so you can eat accordingly would be nice, it's difficult to tell without a number of tests. One risk factor is a family history of high cholesterol and heart disease. However, if you can munch on high cholesterol foods, and blood tests taken soon thereafter reveal no change in blood cholesterol level, you may not need to worry.

This means eggs, labeled a cholesterol pariah (about 213mg per whole egg), may be back on your table. Experts say you're still better off with a low-fat diet with no more than 300mg of cholesterol per day and no more than four yolks a week (whites are okay). Use two whites for each whole egg in a recipe, or use egg substitute.

dish, and cut into 4 equal pieces; set aside, and keep warm.

2. Combine pineapple juice and cornstarch in a 1-cup glass measure; stir well. Microwave at HIGH 1½ minutes or until thick and bubbly; stir well. Serve pineapple sauce with ham. Yield: 4 servings (serving size: 3 ounces ham and 2 tablespoons sauce).

Selections: 3 P/M; **Points:** 4
Per serving: CAL 169 (35% from fat); PRO 18.8g; FAT 6.6g (SAT 2.5g); CARB 7.2g; FIB 0g; CHOL 48mg; IRON 1.2mg; SOD 758mg; CALC 14mg

Oven-Fried Pork Chops

4   (6-ounce) lean center-cut loin pork chops
2   tablespoons pineapple juice
1   tablespoon low-sodium soy sauce
¼   teaspoon ground ginger
⅛   teaspoon garlic powder
1   large egg white, lightly beaten
⅓   cup dry breadcrumbs
¼   teaspoon dried Italian seasoning
¼   teaspoon paprika
Dash of garlic powder
Cooking spray

1. Preheat oven to 350°.

2. Trim fat from chops. Combine juice and next 4 ingredients in a bowl; stir well. Combine breadcrumbs, Italian seasoning, paprika, and dash of garlic powder in a shallow dish; stir well. Dip

Serve Oven-Fried Pork Chops with fluffy rice and steamed green beans.

chops in juice mixture, and dredge in bread crumb mixture.

3. Place chops on a broiler pan coated with cooking spray. Bake at 350° for 50 minutes or until tender, turning after 25 minutes. Yield: 4 servings

Selections: 3 P/M, 40 C; **Points:** 5
Per serving: CAL 227 (35% from fat); PRO 27g; FAT 8.8g (s 2.7g); CARB 7.6g; FIB 0.4g; CHOL 72mg; IRON 0.7mg; SC 248mg; CALC 25mg

Sweet Onion-Smothered Hamburgers

Cooking spray
2   cups thinly sliced onion, separated into rings
½   cup chili sauce, divided
2   tablespoons grape jelly
1   pound ground round
¼   cup dry breadcrumbs
1   tablespoon instant minced onion
¼   teaspoon pepper
1   garlic clove, minced
4   (1½-ounce) hamburger buns, split
4   curly leaf lettuce leaves

1. Coat a large nonstick skillet with cooking spray, and place over medium heat until ho Add onion rings; cover and cook 10 minut or until limp and golden, stirring occasionall Reduce heat to low, and stir in ¼ cup chili sau and grape jelly. Cover and cook 5 minutes, sti ring occasionally.

2. Combine remaining ¼ cup chili sauce, bee breadcrumbs, instant minced onion, pepper, an garlic in a large bowl; stir well. Divide beef mi ture into 4 equal portions, shaping each into ½-inch thick patty. Prepare grill or broiler. Plac patties on grill rack or broiler pan coated wit cooking spray, and cook 4 minutes on each sid or until done.

3. Line bottom halves of buns with a lettuce lea top each with a patty, ¼ cup onion mixture, an top half of bun. Yield: 4 servings.

Selections: 1 FR/V, 3 P/M, 2 B, 50 C; **Points:** 9.5
Per serving: CAL 466 (24% from fat); PRO 34.3g; FAT 12.5g (s 3.4g); CARB 54.8g; FIBER 4.2g; CHOL 96mg; IRON 6.5mg; SO 685mg; CALC 151mg

icken Pot Pies

oking spray

cup diced carrot

cup sliced mushrooms

cup chopped celery

cup frozen green peas, thawed

cup minced fresh onion

cups water

(10¾-ounce) cans condensed reduced-fat

reduced-sodium cream of chicken soup,

undiluted

teaspoon pepper

teaspoon dried thyme

cups diced cooked chicken breast

cup self-rising flour

tablespoons chilled stick margarine, cut

into small pieces

cup skim milk

Preheat oven to 425°.

Coat a large nonstick skillet with cooking
ay, and place over medium-high heat until
hot. Add carrot, mushrooms, celery, green peas, and onion; sauté 5 minutes or until vegetables are tender.

3. Combine water, soup, pepper, and thyme in a medium bowl; stir well. Stir in vegetables and chicken. Spoon chicken mixture evenly into 6 (8-ounce) individual round baking dishes coated with cooking spray.

4. Place flour in a small bowl; cut in margarine with a pastry blender or 2 knives until mixture is crumbly. Sprinkle milk, 1 tablespoon at a time, over surface; toss with a fork until moist. Drop dough by level tablespoons onto chicken mixture. Bake at 425° for 15 minutes or until biscuit topping is golden. Yield: 6 servings.

Selections: 1 B, 2 P/M, 1 FA, 40 C; **Points:** 6
Per serving: CAL 281 (22% from fat) ; PRO 24.7g; FAT 6.8g (sat 1.5g); CARB 28.5g; FIB 1.7g; CHOL 61mg; IRON 2.2mg; SOD 716mg; CALC 109mg

We trimmed the fat and streamlined the procedure in our individual Chicken Pot Pies.

Four-Cheese Stuffed Shells

1½ cups 1% low-fat cottage cheese
1   cup fat-free ricotta cheese
½   cup (2 ounces) crumbled blue cheese
2   tablespoons chopped fresh parsley
1   large egg, lightly beaten
Cooking spray
2   teaspoons olive oil
1   cup chopped onion
1   clove garlic, minced
1   (14½-ounce) can no-salt-added stewed tomatoes, undrained and chopped
1   tablespoon dried Italian seasoning
¼   teaspoon salt
16 uncooked jumbo pasta shells
2   tablespoons (½ ounce) finely shredded fresh Parmesan cheese

1. Combine first 5 ingredients in a bowl; stir well, and set aside.

2. Coat a saucepan with cooking spray; add oil, and place over medium-high heat until hot. Add onion and garlic, and sauté until tender. Stir in tomatoes, Italian seasoning, and salt; bring to a boil. Reduce heat, and simmer, uncovered, 15 minutes, stirring occasionally. Remove from h[...] and set aside.

3. Preheat oven to 375°.

4. Cook pasta shells according to package di[...] tions, omitting salt and fat; drain well. Sp[...] cheese mixture evenly into shells. Arrange sh[...] in an 11- x 7-inch baking dish coated with co[...] ing spray. Pour tomato mixture over shells.

5. Cover and bake at 375° for 25 minutes. [...] cover; sprinkle with Parmesan cheese. Bake, [...] covered, an additional 5 minutes. Let stan[...] minutes before serving. Yield: 8 servings.

Selections: 2 B, 50 C; **Points:** 4.5
Per serving: CAL 214 (22% from fat); PRO 16.2g; FAT 5.2g; [...] 2.3g); CARB 26g; FIB 1.1g; CHOL 39mg; IRON 2.1mg; [...] 403mg; CALC 177mg

Cowboy Steak and Beans

1   pound lean, boned top sirloin steak
2   teaspoons ground cumin
1   teaspoon chili powder
¼   teaspoon ground red pepper
Cooking spray

Four-Cheese Stuffed Shells

½ cups chopped onion
½ cups chopped green bell pepper
  garlic cloves, minced
  cup fat-free beef broth
  tablespoons brown sugar
  (15-ounce) can no-salt-added pinto beans,
  drained
½ cups quartered cherry tomatoes

Trim fat from steak; cut steak into 4 pieces.
ombine cumin, chili powder, and red pepper;
orinkle half of mixture over meat. Coat a non-
ick skillet with cooking spray, and place over
edium heat. Add meat, and cook 5 minutes on
ach side. Remove from skillet; set aside, and
eep warm.

Add onion, bell pepper, and garlic to skillet;
uté until tender. Add remaining cumin mix-
re, broth, sugar, and beans; bring to a boil. Re-
uce heat, and simmer, uncovered, 5 minutes,
irring occasionally. Stir in tomatoes. Arrange
eat over bean mixture. Cover and simmer 5
inutes. Yield: 4 servings.

elections: 1 B, 3 P/M, 1 FR/V; **Points:** 6
er serving: CAL 333 (19% from fat); PRO 32.5g; FAT 7.2g (sat
3g); CARB 35g; FIB 5.5g; CHOL 69mg; IRON 7.1mg; SOD 88mg;
ALC 65mg

esto-Plum Tomato Pizza

e sure to purchase a good quality pesto basil sauce.
lthough it may cost a little more, the difference will
e noticeable.

  (14.5-ounce) package focaccia (Italian
  flatbread) or 1 (1-pound) Italian
  cheese-flavored thin pizza crust (such
  as Boboli)
  tablespoons pesto basil sauce (such as Pesto
  Sanremo)
  pound plum tomatoes, sliced
  garlic cloves, thinly sliced
  cup (2 ounces) preshredded part-skim
  mozzarella cheese
  cup (1⅓ ounces) preshredded fresh
  Parmesan cheese
  teaspoon coarsely ground pepper
  tablespoons thinly sliced fresh basil leaves

. Preheat oven to 450°.

. Place crust on a large baking sheet. Spread

pesto basil sauce evenly over crust, and arrange
tomato and garlic slices over crust. Top with
shredded cheeses, and sprinkle with pepper. Bake
pizza at 450° for 8 minutes or until cheese melts.
Remove from oven, and sprinkle with fresh basil.
Cut pizza into 8 slices. Yield: 4 servings (serving
size: 2 slices).

Selections: 4 B, 1 FA, 1 FR/V, 1 P/M; **Points:** 8
Per serving: CAL 388 (29% from fat); PRO 17.9g; FAT 12.4g (sat
5.3g); CARB 56.5g; FIB 5.6g; CHOL 14mg; IRON 1.5mg; SOD
794mg; CALC 253mg

Hamburger-Mushroom Pizza

This recipe is super quick and easy. You don't
even have to brown the ground beef before topping
the pizza.

1   (16-ounce) loaf unsliced Italian bread
½   cup bottled traditional pizza sauce
8   (⅛-inch-thick) slices onion, separated
    into rings
1   cup presliced fresh mushrooms
6   ounces ultra-lean ground beef
1   teaspoon dried Italian seasoning
½   teaspoon garlic powder
¼   teaspoon crushed red pepper
1½ cups (6 ounces) preshredded pizza
    double-cheese (a blend of part-skim
    mozzarella and cheddar cheese)

1. Preheat oven to 500°.

2. Cut Italian bread loaf in half horizontally.
Place both halves of bread, cut side up, on a large
baking sheet. Spread ¼ cup pizza sauce over each
half of bread. Divide onion rings and sliced
mushrooms evenly between bread halves. Crumble ground beef into ½ inch pieces, and divide
beef evenly between bread halves. Sprinkle Italian
seasoning, garlic powder, and crushed red pepper
evenly over each pizza; top each with ¾ cup
shredded cheese.

3. Bake pizza halves at 500° for 9 minutes or until
ground beef is done and cheese melts. Cut each
pizza half into 3 equal pieces. Yield: 6 servings
(serving size: 1 piece).

Selections: 3 B, 1 FR/V, 2 P/M; **Points:** 6
Per serving: CAL 301 (29% from fat); PRO 15.1g; FAT 9.7g (sat
2.7g); CARB 35.4g; FIB 2g; CHOL 31mg; IRON 2mg; SOD 542mg;
CALC 155mg

A Garden Of Good Health

SALADS OFFER A SMART WAY TO TOSS TOGETHER
A NUTRITIOUS MEAL OF COLOR AND VARIETY.

It's hard to believe but King Louis XIV of France, the embodiment of ostentation, had a weakness for salads. His love of ornate golden decor, which covered his palace in Versailles, earned him the nickname Sun King, a nod to the brilliance of his court. With that regal attitude, you would imagine him dining on flaky, buttery croissants and foods drenched in rich, fatty sauces. This is France after all. But Louis was no dummy. Even in the mid-1600s he knew salads give your body fresh food that is colorful and varied.

Fifty percent of women do not consume even two-thirds of the recommended daily allowance for folic acid, iron, zinc, calcium, magnesium, copper, vitamins E, A, and D, and many B vitamins. To combat diseases such as cancer and attain a healthy weight, you need to eat five servings of fruits and vegetables every day; to reap the most antioxidant and phytonutrient benefits, those foods should be a rainbow of colors. Salads are a smart choice, and this chapter includes a mix of leafy greens, vegetables, and beans. You might not earn a gold crown for eating these, but you just might put a regal step in your gait.

Caesar Salad is said to have been created in 1924 by Caesar Cardini, an Italian chef.

3. Combine bread cubes, lettuce, and cheese in a large bowl; set aside. Combine water and next 7 ingredients in a blender; process until smooth. Pour over salad; toss well. Yield: 4 servings (serving size: 2 cups).

Selections: 1 B, 2 FR/V, 1 FA; **Points:** 3
Per serving: CAL 149 (34% from fat); PRO 6.9g; FAT 5.6g (sat 1.7g); CARB 17.8g; FIB 2.4g; CHOL 5mg; IRON 1.8mg; SOD 460mg; CALC 141mg

Old-fashioned Potato Salad

9   cups cubed red potatoes (about 3 pounds)
½   cup diced onion
½   cup diced celery
¼   cup sweet pickle relish or dill pickle relish, drained
3   hard-cooked large eggs, chopped
1   garlic clove, minced
¾   cup low-fat sour cream
⅓   cup fat-free mayonnaise
2   tablespoons chopped fresh parsley
1   teaspoon dry mustard
¾   teaspoon salt
¼   teaspoon pepper

1. Place potatoes in a Dutch oven; cover with water, and bring to a boil. Cook 8 minutes or until tender. Drain; place in a large bowl. Add onion and next 4 ingredients; toss gently.
2. Combine sour cream and next 5 ingredients in a bowl; stir well. Pour over potato salad; toss gently to coat. Cover and chill. Yield: 9 servings (serving size: 1 cup).

Selections: 1 B, 90 C; **Points:** 4
Per serving: CAL 192 (21% from fat); PRO 6.1g; FAT 4.4g (sat 2.1g); CARB 32.8g; FIB 2.8g; CHOL 78mg; IRON 1.5mg; SOD 383mg; CALC 49mg

Minted Cucumber Salad

½   cup vanilla low-fat yogurt
3   tablespoons chopped fresh mint
2   tablespoons white wine vinegar
2   teaspoons sugar
Dash of hot sauce
3   medium cucumbers, peeled and thinly sliced
1   small red onion, sliced and separated into rings
Boston lettuce leaves (optional)

Rich and creamy Old-fashioned Potato Salad is a natural at any picnic or cookout.

Caesar Salad

4   (¾-ounce) slices French bread, cut into ¾-inch cubes
2   garlic cloves, crushed
8   cups sliced romaine lettuce
½   cup (1 ounce) shaved fresh Parmesan cheese
3   tablespoons water
3   tablespoons fresh lemon juice
2½ teaspoons olive oil
1   teaspoon Dijon mustard
1   teaspoon low-sodium Worcestershire sauce
1   teaspoon anchovy paste
½   teaspoon sugar
3   garlic cloves

1. Preheat oven to 350°.
2. Combine bread cubes and crushed garlic in a large zip-top plastic bag. Seal bag, and shake to coat bread cubes. Turn bread cube mixture out onto a baking sheet, and arrange bread cubes in a single layer. Bake at 350° for 15 minutes or until toasted.

Combine yogurt, chopped mint, white wine
￼egar, sugar, and hot sauce in a shallow dish;
￼ well. Add sliced cucumbers and onion; stir
￼l. Cover and chill at least 30 minutes. Serve
￼ lettuce leaves, if desired. Yield: 6 servings
￼rving size: 1 cup).

￼ections: 1 FR/V; Points: 1
￼ serving: CAL 43 (8% from fat); PRO 1.7g; FAT 0.4g (sat 0.2g);
￼RB 8.8g; FIB 1.4g; CHOL 1mg; IRON 0.3mg; SOD 16mg; CALC
￼g

￼ssed Salad With Creamy
￼ttermilk Dressing

￼ cups torn romaine lettuce
￼ cups torn curly leaf lettuce
￼ cups halved cherry tomatoes
￼ cup sliced red onion
￼ cup chopped celery
￼eamy Buttermilk Dressing

￼ Combine first 5 ingredients in a large bowl,
￼d toss well. Spoon Creamy Buttermilk Dress-
￼ evenly over salad, and toss gently to coat.
￼ve immediately. Yield: 6 servings (serving
￼e: ½ cup).

￼eamy Buttermilk Dressing:
￼ cup low-fat buttermilk
￼ tablespoons fat-free mayonnaise
￼ tablespoon grated Parmesan cheese
￼ teaspoon dried parsley flakes

¼ teaspoon cracked pepper
1 garlic clove, minced

1. Combine all ingredients in a small bowl; stir
well. Yield: about 14 tablespoons.

Selections: 1 FR/V; Points: 1
Per serving: CAL 42 (11% from fat); PRO 2.1g; FAT 0.5g (sat
0.3g); CARB 7.8g; FIB 1.3g; CHOL 1mg; IRON 0.7mg; SOD
239mg; CALC 57mg

Colorful Coleslaw

8 cups thinly sliced green cabbage
1½ cups frozen whole-kernel corn,
    thawed
1 cup shredded carrot
1 cup chopped red onion
1 cup chopped red bell pepper
½ cup sugar
½ cup white vinegar
2 tablespoons water
1 tablespoon vegetable oil
1 teaspoon celery seeds
½ teaspoon salt
½ teaspoon chicken-flavored bouillon
    granules
¼ teaspoon white pepper
¼ teaspoon mustard seeds
Dash of hot sauce

1. Combine first 5 ingredients in a large bowl,
and toss well.
2. Combine sugar and next 9 ingredients in a
small saucepan; bring mixture to a boil, stirring

**Tossed Salad With
Creamy Buttermilk
Dressing tastes so fresh
and is so simple to make
you might abandon
bottled dressings.**

￼OW TO PREPARE AND
￼TORE SALAD GREENS

￼o clean tight heads of greens such as iceberg lettuce and
￼abbage, begin by removing the core. Then run cool water into
￼he core end of the head and over the leaves; invert the head
￼o drain.
￼ To clean leafy greens such as romaine or spinach, remove the
￼eaves from the stems; place in a sink full of cool water. Gently
￼wish the greens before removing them from the water to drain.
￼ The crisper drawer in the refrigerator maintains the ideal
￼umidity for storing salad greens. When prepared as directed
￼bove, tender greens such as spinach and leaf lettuce will stay
￼resh for four to five days. Firmer greens such as iceberg lettuce
￼nd green cabbage will stay fresh for up to three weeks.

UNCORK THE VIRTUES OF VINEGAR

Lots of flavor, no fat. With that winning combination, a bottle of flavored vinegar is worth the extra cost at the supermarket or the short time it takes to make your own.

It's a flavor secret professional cooks have used for years—a splash of raspberry vinegar in salad dressings, a spoonful of herbed vinegar in beef stew. Until recently, flavored vinegars seemed too "gourmet" for the average cook. You could buy them only from cooks' catalogs or specialty food shops. But now the secret's out. Fruit and herb vinegars line the shelves in most grocery stores. You pay a little more than for regular distilled vinegars, but the flavor is worth it. Once flavored vinegars become a staple in your kitchen, you'll want to make your own because you'll save money and the process can take as little as 10 minutes. (See the box at right for directions.)

constantly until sugar dissolves. Pour over coleslaw; toss well.

3. Cover and chill at least 2 hours. Stir before serving; serve with a slotted spoon. Yield: 10 servings (serving size: 1 cup).

Selections: 1 FR/V, 70 C; **Points:** 2
Per serving: CAL 106 (15% from fat); PRO 2.1g; FAT 1.8g (sat 0.3g); CARB 23g; FIB 3.2g; CHOL 0mg; IRON 0.9mg; SOD 178mg; CALC 44mg

Simple Fruit Salad

¼ cup pineapple juice
1½ tablespoons honey
1 tablespoon lemon juice
1 teaspoon grated orange rind
¼ teaspoon ground ginger
1 cup coarsely chopped apple
1 cup coarsely chopped pear
1 cup sliced plums
1 cup sliced banana

1. Combine first 5 ingredients in a large bowl, and stir with a whisk until well blended. Add apple, pear, plums, and banana; toss gently to coat. Serve immediately. Yield: 7 servings (serving size: ½ cup).

Selections: 1 FR/V; **Points:** 1
Per serving: CAL 70 (5% from fat); PRO 0.5g; FAT 0.4g (sat 0.1g); CARB 18g; FIB 2g; CHOL 0mg; IRON 0.2mg; SOD 1mg; CALC 8mg

Fruit-and-Honey Spinach Salad

8 cups fresh spinach leaves
2 cups cantaloupe balls
1½ cups halved strawberries
2 tablespoons seedless raspberry jam
2 tablespoons raspberry vinegar
1 tablespoon honey
2 teaspoons olive oil
¼ cup chopped macadamia nuts

1. Combine spinach leaves, cantaloupe balls, and strawberry halves in a large bowl; toss gently. Combine raspberry jam, raspberry vinegar, honey, and oil in a small bowl; stir with a whisk until blended. Drizzle over salad; toss well. Sprinkle with chopped nuts. Yield: 6 servings (serving size: 1⅓ cups).

Three-Bean Salad

Selections: 1 FA, 2 FR/V, 30 C; **Points:** 2
Per serving: CAL 128 (44% from fat); PRO 3.3g; FAT 6.3g (sat 1g); CARB 17.7g; FIB 4.7g; CHOL 0mg; IRON 2.4mg; SOD 67mg; CALC 88mg

Three-Bean Salad

1   (16-ounce) can no-salt-added green beans, drained
1   (16-ounce) can wax beans, drained
1   (16-ounce) can kidney beans, drained
1   cup chopped green bell pepper
⅔   cup chopped green onions
⅔   cup apple juice
⅓   cup cider vinegar
2   teaspoons sugar
½   teaspoon pepper
¼   teaspoon dry mustard
¼   teaspoon paprika
⅛   teaspoon dried oregano

1. Combine first 5 ingredients in a large bowl, and toss gently.

2. Combine apple juice and next 6 ingredients in a small jar; cover tightly, and shake vigorously. Pour vinaigrette over salad; toss gently. Cover and chill at least 2 hours. Yield 12 servings (serving size: ½ cup).

Selections: 1 FR/V, 30 C; **Points:** 1
Per serving: CAL 55 (5% from fat); PRO 2.8g; FAT 0.3g (sat 0); CARB 11.3g; FIB 1.8g; CHOL 0mg; IRON 1.4mg; SOD 56mg; CALC 25mg

Making Flavored Vinegars

Follow these four simple steps for making your own flavored vinegars.

1. Wash jars thoroughly. Rinse; dry completely.

2. Fill jars with clean, dry herbs or fruit. Pour white wine vinegar over herbs or fruit. Cover with lids; let stand 2 weeks.

3. Pour aged vinegar through wire-mesh strainer lined with 2 layers of cheesecloth into a bowl.

4. Pour strained vinegar into clean decorative bottles or jars. Add fresh herbs or fruit to jars, if desired. Seal bottles with a cork or lid.

Second in Command

B*ridesmaid. Vice president. Talk-show host sidekick. Backup singer to Barbra Streisand. They all have something in common: They're always outshined by a more traditional presence. And it doesn't just happen in show biz and politics. A little attention inequity takes place in the kitchen as well. Consider those fresh, colorful dishes that are usually afterthoughts to the baked chicken, the lasagna, the pork medallions. From a health standpoint, side dishes are the most important meal component because that's typically where the cook puts the fresh vegetables.*

Only about 22% of Americans eat daily the recommended five servings of vegetables and fruit, key tools in fighting diseases such as cancer and heart disease. Aside from being healthful, side dishes such as Sesame Asparagus and Roasted Rosemary Potatoes can hold their own, flavorwise, against any entrée, and they're practically effortless to prepare. It's enough to make you reconsider what gets top billing in the center of your plate and what is relegated to the rim.

Rice vinegar and sesame lend Oriental flavor to Sesame Asparagus.

Sesame Asparagus

1¼ pounds asparagus spears
2 tablespoons rice vinegar
1 tablespoon water
1 teaspoon dark sesame oil
1 teaspoon lemon juice
1½ teaspoons sesame seeds

1. Snap off tough ends of asparagus; remove scales with a knife or vegetable peeler, if desired. Steam asparagus, covered, 4 minutes or until crisp-tender. Place asparagus in a large, shallow dish.

2. Combine vinegar, water, oil, and juice; stir well. Pour over asparagus; toss gently to coat. Sprinkle with sesame seeds. Yield: 6 servings.

Selections: 1 FR/V; **Points:** 0
Per serving: CAL 25 (47% from fat); PRO 2.1g; FAT 1.3g (sat 0.2g); CARB 2.5g; FIB 1.3g; CHOL 0mg; IRON 0.6mg; SOD 2mg; CALC 14mg

Brown Rice Pilaf

½ cup diced carrot
½ cup diced red bell pepper
3 cups water
1 cup uncooked brown rice
½ teaspoon salt
½ teaspoon dried oregano
½ teaspoon dried thyme
2 large garlic cloves, minced

1. Steam carrot and bell pepper, covered, 2 minutes or until crisp-tender. Drain well; set aside.

2. Combine water and next 5 ingredients in a saucepan; bring to a boil. Cover, reduce heat, and simmer 45 minutes. Stir in carrot-bell pepper mixture; cover and cook an additional 5 minutes or until rice is tender and liquid is absorbed. Fluff with a fork. Yield: 8 servings (serving size: ½ cup).

Selections: 1 B; **Points:** 2
Per serving: CAL 93 (7% from fat); PRO 2.1g; FAT 0.7g (sat 0.2g); CARB 19.6g; FIB 1.3g; CHOL 0mg; IRON 0.7mg; SOD 152mg; CALC 13mg

Lemon Broccoli

1½ pounds broccoli
1 teaspoon grated lemon rind
⅛ teaspoon salt
⅛ teaspoon pepper
Lemon rind curls (optional)

1. Trim off large leaves of broccoli; remove to ends of lower stalks. Cut into spears. Steam br coli spears, covered, 5 minutes or until crisp-t der. Place broccoli spears on a platter; sprin with grated lemon rind, salt, and pepper. Garr with lemon rind curls, if desired. Yield: 6 servi

Selections: 1 FR/V; **Points:** 0
Per serving: CAL 25 (11% from fat); PRO 2.7g; FAT 0.3g (sat 0
Per serving: CARB 4.6g; FIB 2.3g; CHOL 0mg; IRON 0.8mg;
72mg; CALC 42mg

Poached Pears With Blue Chee and Toasted Walnuts

4 firm ripe Bartlett pears
1 cup water
½ cup dry red wine
¼ cup fresh lemon juice
½ cup (2 ounces) crumbled blue cheese
2½ tablespoons coarsely chopped walnuts, toasted
Watercress sprigs (optional)
Freshly ground pepper (optional)

1. Peel and core pears; cut each in half lengthw Combine water, wine, and lemon juice in a ski bring to a boil. Place pear halves, cut sides do in skillet. Cover, reduce heat, and simmer 20 m utes, turning and basting once with wine mixtu

2. Remove pears from skillet; discard wine m ture. Place pear halves on a serving platter; sp kle cheese and walnuts evenly over each pear h Garnish with watercress sprigs, and sprinkle w pepper, if desired. Yield: 8 servings.

Poached Pears With Blue Cheese and Toasted Walnuts

Selections: 1 FR/V, 30 C; **Points:** 2
Per serving: CAL 102 (36% from fat); PRO 2.6g; FAT 4.1g (sat 1.5g); CARB 15.7g; FIB 2.8g; CHOL 5mg; IRON 0.4mg; SOD 99mg; CALC 50mg

Green Bean Casserole

Cooking spray
¼ cup finely chopped onion
2 tablespoons all-purpose flour
1 cup skim milk
½ cup (2 ounces) shredded reduced-fat, reduced-sodium Swiss cheese
1 teaspoon sugar
½ teaspoon salt
½ cup low-fat sour cream
2 (9-ounce) packages frozen French-style green beans, thawed and drained
1½ cups herb-seasoned stuffing mix
2 teaspoons margarine, melted
1 large egg white, lightly beaten

1. Preheat oven to 350°.

2. Coat a medium saucepan with cooking spray, and place over medium heat until hot. Add onion, and sauté 5 minutes or until tender. Add flour, and cook 1 minute, stirring constantly. Gradually add milk, stirring with a whisk until blended. Stir in cheese, sugar, and salt; cook 5 minutes or until thick and bubbly, stirring constantly. Remove from heat; stir in sour cream.

3. Place green beans in an 8-inch square baking dish, and pour sauce over green beans. Combine stuffing mix, margarine, and egg white in a bowl; stir well, and sprinkle stuffing mixture over green bean mixture. Bake at 350° for 25 minutes or until thoroughly heated. Yield: 8 servings (serving size: ½ cup).

Selections: 1 FA, 80 C; **Points:** 3
Per serving: CAL 139 (30% from fat); PRO 6.9g; FAT 4.7g (sat 2.1g); CARB 18.7g; FIB 2.1g; CHOL 11mg; IRON 0.8mg; SOD 382mg; CALC 169mg

Fresh Beets in Orange Sauce

1½ pounds medium beets
2 teaspoons cornstarch
½ cup orange juice
1½ tablespoons reduced-calorie stick margarine
1 teaspoon sugar
1 teaspoon grated orange rind
1 teaspoon cider vinegar
¼ teaspoon salt

Herb-seasoned stuffing mix makes a low-fat topping for Green Bean Casserole.

Green Beans With Bacon-
Balsamic Vinaigrette

Leave root and 1 inch of stem on beets; scrub ith a brush. Place in a saucepan; add water to ver. Bring to a boil; cover. Reduce heat; simmer 5 minutes or until tender. Drain; rinse under ld water. Drain; let cool slightly. Trim off beet ots; rub off skins. Cut beets into ¼-inch slices.

Combine cornstarch and juice; stir well. Set ide. Melt margarine in a saucepan over medium eat. Add orange juice mixture, sugar, and next 3 gredients; cook until thick and bubbly, stirring nstantly. Add beets; reduce heat to low. Cook 3 inutes or until thoroughly heated, stirring con- antly. Yield: 5 servings (serving size: ½ cup).

lections: 1 FR/V, 1 FA; **Points:** 1
r serving: CAL 61 (38% from fat); PRO 1g; FAT 2.6g (sat 0.3g); RB 10g; FIB 0.9g; CHOL 0mg; IRON 0.7mg; SOD 189mg; LC 16mg

reen Beans With Bacon- alsamic Vinaigrette

    pounds green beans
    bacon slices
    cup minced shallots
    tablespoons coarsely chopped almonds
    tablespoons brown sugar
    cup white balsamic vinegar

Cook beans in boiling water for 2 minutes. rain; rinse under cold water. Drain well; set aside.

Cook bacon over medium-high heat until crisp.

Remove bacon; crumble. Set aside. Add shallots to bacon fat in skillet; sauté 1 minute. Add almonds; sauté 1 minute. Remove skillet from heat; let cool slightly. Add sugar and vinegar to skillet; stir until sugar dissolves. Stir in crumbled bacon.

3. Pour vinaigrette over beans, tossing gently to coat. Yield: 8 servings (serving size: ¾ cup).

Selections: 1 FR/V, 40 C; **Points:** 1
Per serving: CAL 75 (31% from fat); PRO 3.4g; FAT 2.6g (sat 0.5g); CARB 11.8g; FIB 2.8g; CHOL 0mg; IRON 1.4mg; SOD 50mg; CALC 54mg

Quick Succotash

½   cup water
1   (10-ounce) package frozen baby lima
     beans, thawed
1   (10-ounce) package frozen whole-kernel
     corn, thawed
¾   cup diced green bell pepper
½   teaspoon salt
¼   teaspoon dried summer savory, crushed
2   cups diced seeded peeled tomato

1. Bring ½ cup water to a boil in a saucepan. Add beans; cook, uncovered, 5 minutes. Add corn and next 3 ingredients; cook 5 minutes, stirring occa- sionally. Remove from heat; stir in tomato. Yield: 5 servings (serving size: 1cup).

Selections: 1 B, 1 FR/V; **Points:** 2
Per serving: CAL 143 (3% from fat); PRO 7g; FAT 0.5g (sat 0.1g); CARB 31g; FIB 4g; CHOL 0mg; IRON 2.4mg; SOD 328mg; CALC 31mg

Quick Succotash is a southern United States favorite.

FIBER OPTIONS

Fiber lowers cholesterol levels, helps you lose weight, and may even prevent cancer. The catch is that you need to consume a lot of it—20 to 35 grams daily. But have no fear. There's plenty of soluble and insoluble fiber in the foods you love. Soluble fiber (in fruits, vegetables, legumes, oats, barley, brown rice, and seeds) is the cholesterol-lowering hero that absorbs liquid and swells to form a sticky gel that traps and removes cholesterol from the body. Insoluble fiber is the part of fruits, vegetables, and whole grains that isn't digested and moves everything through the digestive tract, reducing the risk of colorectal cancer.

To avoid intestinal problems, build up your fiber intake gradually. Add about five grams of fiber each week until you reach at least 20 grams. Drink 8 to 10 glasses of water daily as you increase your fiber intake to help move it through your system.

To add more flavor to vegetables, roast them in your oven. Roasting vegetables—carrots, garlic, onions, peppers, potatoes, tomatoes, for example—concentrates their flavors and brings out their natural sweetness. Roasted root vegetables make a great topping for rice or, when puréed, a wonderful sauce for meats.

Cut vegetables into uniform pieces before roasting. Root vegetables such as carrots, potatoes, and turnips can be parboiled first to reduce roasting time. To parboil, immerse the vegetables in boiling water for 2 minutes; then drain and let cool. To roast, spread vegetables in a single layer on a baking sheet and then coat with cooking spray. Most vegetables take 10 to 20 minutes at 400° to 450° to roast, but root vegetables, onions, and garlic need 30 to 40 minutes to roast while being stirred occasionally.

Roasted Vidalias

4   medium Vidalia or other sweet onions (about 2 pounds), each peeled and cut into 8 wedges
Olive oil-flavored cooking spray
1   teaspoon dried thyme
½   teaspoon salt
¼   teaspoon freshly ground pepper
1   tablespoon balsamic vinegar

1. Preheat oven to 350°.

2. Arrange onion wedges, flat side down, on a jelly-roll pan coated with cooking spray; lightly coat onions with cooking spray. Sprinkle thyme, salt, and pepper over onions. Bake at 350° for 30 minutes. Turn onions over; bake an additional 25 minutes. Spoon onions into a serving dish; drizzle with vinegar. Yield: 4 servings (serving size: ¾ cup).

Selections: 1 FR/V; **Points:** .5
Per serving: CAL 57 (6% from fat); PRO 1.7g; FAT 0.4g (sat 0.1g); CARB 12.6g; FIB 2.7g; CHOL 0mg; IRON 0.8mg; SOD 297mg; CALC 36mg

Glazed Sweet Potatoes

1   pound sweet potatoes, peeled
Cooking spray
1   tablespoon cornstarch
¾   cup orange juice
1   tablespoon brown sugar
2   tablespoons lemon juice

1. Preheat oven to 425°.

2. Cut sweet potatoes into ½-inch-thick slices; place in a 1-quart casserole coated with cooking spray. Combine cornstarch and next 3 ingredients in a bowl; stir well. Pour over potatoes. Cover; bake at 425° for 45 minutes or until potatoes are tender. Yield: 5 servings (serving size: ½ cup).

Selections: 1 B; **Points:** 2
Per serving: CAL 110 (3% from fat); PRO 1.5g; FAT 0.4g (sat 0.1g); CARB 25.7g; FIB 2.3g; CHOL 0mg; IRON 0.5mg; SOD 11mg; CALC 22mg

Cheesy Squash Casserole

2   pounds yellow squash, sliced
¾   cup chopped onion
1   tablespoon reduced-calorie stick margarine
2   tablespoons all-purpose flour
1   cup skim milk
¾   cup (3 ounces) shredded reduced-fat cheddar cheese
½   teaspoon salt
¼   teaspoon pepper
Cooking spray
½   cup fresh breadcrumbs, toasted

1. Preheat oven to 350°.

2. Steam squash and onion, covered, 12 minut or until tender. Drain; set aside.

3. Melt margarine in a saucepan over mediu heat. Add flour; cook 1 minute, stirring co stantly. Gradually add milk; cook until mixture thick and bubbly, stirring constantly. Remo from heat; add cheese, salt, and pepper, stirri until cheese melts. Stir in squash-onion mixture

Spoon squash mixture into a shallow 1½-quart asserole coated with cooking spray; sprinkle ith breadcrumbs. Bake at 350° for 20 minutes r until thoroughly heated. Yield: 8 servings.

elections: 1 FR/V, 70 C; **Points:** 2
r serving: CAL 95 (32% from fat); PRO 6.2g; FAT 3.4g (sat 1.4g); ARB 8.3g; FIB 2.2g; CHOL 8mg; IRON 0.8mg; SOD 277mg; ALC 149mg

affron Rice

Cooking spray
- cup chopped onion
- garlic clove, minced
- cup uncooked long-grain rice
- ⅓ cups fat-free chicken broth
- teaspoon salt
- teaspoon ground saffron

1. Coat a saucepan with cooking spray; place over medium-high heat until hot. Add onion and garlic; sauté until tender. Add rice; sauté 1 minute, stirring constantly. Stir in chicken broth, salt, and saffron. Bring to a boil; cover. Reduce heat, and simmer 20 minutes or until rice is tender and liquid is absorbed. Yield: 4 servings (serving size: ½ cup).

Selections: 1 B; **Points:** 2.5
Per serving: CAL 129 (3% from fat); PRO 2g; FAT .4g (sat .1g); CARB 27g; FIB 1g; CHOL 0mg; IRON 1.4mg; SOD 150mg; CALC 12mg

Roasted Rosemary Potatoes

- 24 small red potatoes (about 2 pounds), each cut in half
- 1 tablespoon olive oil
- 1¼ teaspoons dried rosemary, crushed

Roasted Vidalias make a savory accompaniment to grilled fish, poultry, or steak.

¼　teaspoon salt
¼　teaspoon dried thyme
⅛　teaspoon pepper
Cooking spray

1. Preheat oven to 375°.

2. Combine all ingredients except cooking spray in a bowl; toss to coat. Place potato halves in a single layer on a jelly-roll pan coated with cooking spray. Bake at 375° for 55 minutes or until tender and lightly browned. Yield: 6 servings (serving size: 8 potato halves).

Selections: 1 B, 1 FA; **Points:** 2.5
Per serving: CAL 143 (16% from fat); PRO 3.6g; FAT 2.6g (sat 0.4g); CARB 27.3g; FIB 3.0g; CHOL 0mg; IRON 2.3mg; SOD 109mg; CALC 25mg

Potato Gratin

1　clove garlic, halved
Cooking spray
1　cup chopped onion
6　medium-size baking potatoes, peeled and cut into ⅛-inch slices (about 2½ pounds)

¼　teaspoon salt
¼　teaspoon freshly ground pepper
¾　cup (3 ounces) shredded extra-sharp cheddar cheese
¼　cup grated fresh Romano cheese
1¾ cups low-sodium chicken broth
1　cup evaporated skimmed milk

1. Rub a shallow 3-quart baking dish with cu▮ sides of garlic halves; discard garlic. Coat dish with cooking spray.

2. Coat a small nonstick skillet with cooking spray, and place over medium heat until hot. Add onion, and sauté 5 minutes or until onion is tender; set aside.

3. Arrange one-third of potato slices in prepared dish, and sprinkle with half of salt and half of pepper. Top with half of sautéed onion and half of cheddar and Romano cheeses. Repeat layers, ending with the remaining potato slices.

4. Bring broth and milk to a boil over low heat i▮

small saucepan; pour over potato mixture.
ake, uncovered, at 425° for 50 minutes or until
nder. Let stand 5 minutes before serving. Yield:
servings (serving size: 1 cup).

lections: 1 B, 1 P/M, 50 C; **Points:** 5
r serving: CAL 245 (25% from fat); PRO 12.2g; FAT 6.9g (sat
); CARB 34.3g; FIB 2.9g; CHOL 21mg; IRON 1mg; SOD 323mg;
LC 294mg

ld-fashioned Baked Beans

    (16-ounce) package dried navy beans
2 quarts water
    cups chopped onion
    cup reduced-calorie ketchup
    cup chopped lean ham
    cup molasses
    tablespoon prepared mustard
    teaspoon salt
    teaspoon pepper
    ooking spray

Sort and wash beans; place beans in a Dutch
ven. Cover with water to 2 inches above beans;
ver. Let stand 8 hours. Drain and return to pan.

Add 1½ quarts water and onion to pan; bring
a boil. Cover, reduce heat, and simmer 2 hours.
rain beans, reserving 2 cups cooking liquid.

Preheat oven to 350°.

Combine bean mixture, reserved cooking liq-
d, ketchup, and next 5 ingredients in a large
owl; stir well. Spoon mixture into a 3-quart

casserole coated with cooking spray. Bake, uncovered, at 350° for 1½ hours or until beans are tender. Yield: 15 servings (serving size: ½ cup).

Selections: 2 P/M; **Points:** 2
Per serving: CAL 150 (4% from fat); PRO 8g; FAT 0.7g (sat 0.2g);
CARB 28.2g; FIB 3.4g; CHOL 2mg; IRON 2.6mg; SOD 171mg;
CALC 75mg

Creamy Garlic Potatoes

4   cups cubed peeled baking potato
½   cup skim milk
½   cup plain fat-free yogurt
½   teaspoon salt
4   garlic cloves, minced
2   tablespoons minced fresh chives

1. Place potato in a saucepan; cover with water,
and bring to a boil. Reduce heat, and simmer 30
minutes or until tender; drain. Return potato to
pan. Add milk, yogurt, salt, and garlic; beat at
medium speed of a mixer until smooth. Stir in
chives. Yield: 8 servings (serving size: ½ cup).

Selections: 1 B; **Points:** 1
Per serving: CAL 83 (1% from fat); PRO 3.2g; FAT 0.1g (sat 0.1g);
CARB 17.6g; FIB 1.4g; CHOL 1mg; IRON 0.7mg; SOD 171mg;
CALC 57mg

Hash Brown Casserole

Cooking spray
1½ cups chopped onion
3   tablespoons all-purpose flour

As it bakes,
**Old-fashioned Baked
Beans** fills the house
with an enticing aroma.

TIPS FOR OLD-FASHIONED
BAKED BEANS

Before cooking, carefully sort through the dried beans to
remove and discard any rocks or darkened or blemished beans
that may have been overlooked during packaging.

• To keep the fat content low, our recipe for Old-fashioned
Baked Beans uses lean cooked ham, which provides a traditional smoky flavor.

• You can test the baked beans for doneness in one of two
ways: Either spear a couple of beans with a fork, or press
1 or 2 cooled beans between your fingers to feel how tender
they are.

• If you don't have dried navy beans on hand, Great Northern
beans can be substituted.

½ teaspoon dry mustard
¼ teaspoon salt
1¼ cups skim milk
½ cup low-salt chicken broth
1½ cups (6 ounces) shredded reduced-fat
    sharp cheddar cheese
¾ cup (3 ounces) shredded Swiss cheese
½ teaspoon pepper
1 cup fat-free sour cream
1 (32-ounce) package frozen Southern-style
    hash brown potatoes, thawed
Paprika

1. Preheat oven to 350°.

2. Coat a medium saucepan with cooking spray; place over medium heat until hot. Add onion; sauté 3 minutes or until tender. Stir in flour, mustard, and salt; cook 1 minute. Remove from heat; gradually add milk and broth, stirring constantly with a whisk until blended. Cook over medium heat 5 minutes or until thick, stirring constantly. Remove from heat; add cheeses and pepper, stirring until cheeses melt. Stir in sour cream.

3. Combine cheese mixture and potatoes; stir well. Spoon into 13- x 9-inch baking dish coated with cooking spray. Sprinkle with paprika. Cover, and bake at 350° for 35 minutes. Uncover, and bake an additional 35 minutes. Yield: 8 servings (serving size: 1 cup).

Selections: 1 B, 1 P/M, 80 C; **Points:** 5
Per serving: CAL 247 (27% from fat); PRO 14.8g; FAT 7.4g (sat 4.3g); CARB 29.5g; FIB 1.2g; CHOL 25mg; IRON 1.1mg; SOD 309mg; CALC 357mg

Easy Corn Casserole

Easy Corn Casserole

¼ cup egg substitute
¼ cup reduced-calorie stick margarine,
    melted
1 (8¾-ounce) can no-salt-added whole-
    kernel corn, drained
1 (8¾-ounce) can no-salt-added cream-style
    corn
1 (8½-ounce) package corn muffin mix
1 (8-ounce) carton plain fat-free yogurt
Cooking spray

1. Preheat oven to 350°.

2. Combine first 6 ingredients in a medium bowl; stir well. Pour into an 8-inch square baking dish coated with cooking spray. Bake at 350° for 45 minutes or until set. Yield: 8 servings.

Selections: 2 B, 30 C; **Points:** 5
Per serving: CAL 220 (31% from fat); PRO 5.4g; FAT 7.5g (sat 2.5g); CARB 34.6g; FIB 0.6g; CHOL 1mg; IRON 0.9mg; SOD 287mg; CALC 152mg

Herb-Marinated Tomatoes

2 large tomatoes, cut into ½-inch slices
2 tablespoons chopped fresh basil
1 tablespoon chopped fresh parsley
1 tablespoon chopped fresh oregano
1 tablespoon fresh lemon juice
1 teaspoon balsamic vinegar
¼ teaspoon salt
¼ teaspoon freshly ground pepper

1. Arrange tomato slices on a platter, slightly overlapping. Sprinkle with basil, parsley, and oregano.
2. Combine lemon juice and vinegar; drizzle over tomatoes. Cover and chill 2 hours. Sprinkle with salt and pepper. Yield: 4 servings.

Selections: 1 FR/V; **Points:** .5
Per serving: CAL 39 (16% from fat); PRO 1.6g; FAT 0.7g (sat 0.1g); CARB 8.8g; FIB 1.4g; CHOL 0mg; IRON 1.3mg; SOD 162mg; CALC 28mg

Crispy Oven-Fried Okra

1¾ pounds okra
1½ cups yellow cornmeal
½ teaspoon salt
⅛ teaspoon pepper
½ cup low-fat buttermilk
1 large egg, lightly beaten
Cooking spray

b-Marinated Tomatoes

Stewed Tomatoes and Okra

Preheat oven to 450°.

Trim off stem ends of okra, and cut into ½-ch slices. Combine yellow cornmeal, salt, and pper in a medium bowl; stir mixture well, d set aside.

Combine buttermilk and egg in a large bowl; d okra, stirring to coat. Let stand 10 minutes. rain, and dredge okra in cornmeal mixture. ace okra on a baking sheet coated with cooking ray. Bake at 450° for 40 minutes or until crisp, rring occasionally. Yield: 12 servings (serving e: ½ cup).

ections: 1 B; **Points:** 1
r serving: CAL 84 (12% from fat); PRO 3.1g; FAT 1.1g (sat 0.3g); RB 15.9g; FIB 2.1g; CHOL 19mg; IRON 2.4mg; SOD 123mg; LC 30mg

tewed Tomatoes and Okra

pound fresh okra pods
ooking spray
cup finely chopped onion
cup finely chopped green bell pepper
cups seeded, coarsely chopped unpeeled
tomato (about 3 medium)
tablespoon lemon juice
teaspoon dried oregano
teaspoon salt
teaspoon hot sauce

Remove tip and stem ends from okra; cut okra to ¼-inch slices, and set aside.

2. Coat a medium saucepan with cooking spray, and place over medium heat until hot. Add chopped onion and green bell pepper, and cook 2 minutes, stirring constantly. Add okra slices, chopped tomato, lemon juice, dried oregano, salt, and hot sauce. Cover and cook over medium-low heat 15 minutes or until okra is tender, stirring occasionally. Yield: 3 servings (serving size: 1 cup).

Selections: 1 FR/V; **Points:** 1
Per serving: CAL 80 (10% from fat); PRO 3.4g; FAT 0.9g (sat 0.1g); CARB 16.7g; FIB 3.2g; CHOL 0mg; IRON 1.7mg; SOD 218mg; CALC 99mg

Oven Fries

1½ pounds baking potatoes, peeled and cut into thin strips
1 tablespoon vegetable oil
½ teaspoon salt

1. Preheat oven to 450°.
2. Combine potato strips, vegetable oil, and salt in a large bowl, and toss well. Arrange the potato strips in a single layer on a baking sheet. Bake at 450° for 35 minutes or until fries are golden. Yield: 4 servings.

Selections: 1 B, 1 FA; **Points:** 3.6
Per serving: CAL 193 (17% from fat); PRO 3.3g; FAT 3.6g (sat 0.7g); CARB 36.6g; FIB 2.6g; CHOL 0mg; IRON 0.6mg; SOD 301mg; CALC 9mg

Pair Oven Fries with a grilled burger for America's favorite meal.

SPUD SPECIFICS

One medium-size potato (about 6 ounces) has approximately 180 calories and less than ¼ gram of fat. Besides providing almost half of the adult requirement for vitamin C, 3 grams of fiber, and a reasonable amount of niacin, riboflavin, and thiamine, potatoes contain more potassium than bananas and practically no sodium.

By baking Oven Fries instead of deep-frying them, we've practically eliminated the oil. Our fries have 193 calories and 3.6 grams of fat, while a small order of fries from McDonald's weighs in at 210 calories and 10 grams of fat. If you order large fries, the calories jump to 450 and the fat grams to 22.

The key to getting crispy fries without the fat is to slice them thin. This also creates more surface area for the oil and salt to cover.

A Humble Bowl Of Kinship

THESE SOUPS ALLOW YOU TO FOCUS ON THE COMPANY AND NOURISHMENT—NOT THE KITCHEN.

There is something humble, pure, possibly even sacred about a bowl of soup. The image of one person sitting at a small wooden table with a bowl and spoon represents much about life and nourishment. That image conveys the philosophy that the most rewarding life is one reduced to its most meaningful, elemental components.

In Nigeria, a similar ritual takes on greater significance. The father dines in solitude—a sign of his position in the family. However, the mother and children gather around a generous bowl, usually containing some type of thick soup. It is symbolic of the importance of community, kinship, and closeness.

Regardless of our residency, where and what we eat speaks a lot about us. Soups are so simple in presentation that they allow us to focus on the company and the pleasure of eating. The only problem is that preparation can be a production. Not so with the recipes in this chapter. The ingredients are few, and the pans minimal. Choose from a variety—warm or chilled, savory or sweet—of delicious soups and let your mind focus on the moment rather than solely on the meal.

For brunch, Berry Soup pairs perfectly with chicken salad.

Fresh Corn Chowder comes straight from the garden.

Berry Soup

2   cups raspberries
1   cup sliced strawberries
1   cup orange juice
¼   cup rosé wine
2   tablespoons powdered sugar
1   teaspoon grated orange rind
1   (8-ounce) carton vanilla low-fat yogurt
Fresh mint leaves (optional)

1. Place raspberries and strawberries in a blender or food processor; process until smooth. Strain berry purée through a fine sieve; discard seeds.

2. Return berry purée to blender. Add orange juice and next 4 ingredients, and process until smooth. Pour into a bowl; cover and chill. Ladle into individual bowls; garnish with mint, if desired. Yield: 4 servings (serving size: 1 cup).

Selections: 1 FR/V, 80 C; **Points:** 2
Per serving: CAL 139 (8% from fat:); PRO 4g; FAT 1.2g (sat 0.5g); CARB 27.7g; FIB 5.3g; CHOL 3mg; IRON 0.7mg; SOD 39mg; CALC 122mg

Fresh Corn Chowder

8   ears corn
Cooking spray
1   tablespoon margarine
½   cup finely chopped onion
½   cup thinly sliced celery
1   cup cubed peeled baking potato
1   cup canned vegetable broth
1   cup water
3   tablespoons all-purpose flour
2   cups 1% low-fat milk, divided
2   tablespoons minced fresh thyme
1   teaspoon sugar
¼   teaspoon pepper
½   cup chopped seeded tomato
3   turkey-bacon slices, cooked and crumbled

1. Cut kernels from ears of corn; place in a large bowl. Working over bowl, scrape "milk" and any remaining pulp from cobs using the dull side of a knife blade; set aside.

2. Coat a Dutch oven with cooking spray. Add margarine; place over medium-high heat until

rgarine melts. Add onion and celery; sauté
il tender. Stir in corn, potato, broth, and water;
ng to a boil. Cover, reduce heat, and simmer
minutes or until corn and potato are tender.

Place flour in a bowl; gradually add ½ cup
k, stirring with a whisk until smooth. Add
ur mixture, remaining 1½ cups milk, thyme,
ar, and pepper to vegetable mixture. Cook
r medium heat 4 minutes or until thick and
bly, stirring constantly.

Ladle chowder into individual bowls; top each
ving with tomato and crumbled bacon. Yield:
ervings (serving size: 1½ cups).

ctions: 2 B, 1 FA, 50 C; Points: 4
serving: CAL 253 (19% from fat); PRO 9.7g; FAT 5.4g (sat
); CARB 47.1g; FIB 6.6g; CHOL 5mg; IRON 1.5mg; SOD
mg; CALC 116mg

hite Bean Chili

cup dried Great Northern beans
(14¼-ounce) cans fat-free chicken broth
oking spray
teaspoons vegetable oil
cup chopped onion
cup sliced green onions
garlic cloves, minced
pound ground chicken or turkey breast
cup fresh corn kernels or frozen whole-
kernel corn, thawed
tablespoon chili powder
teaspoon salt
teaspoon ground cumin
(4.5-ounce) can chopped green chiles
tablespoons yellow cornmeal
opped green onions (optional)

Sort and wash beans; place in a large Dutch
n. Cover with water to 2 inches above beans.
ng to a boil; cook 2 minutes. Remove from
t; cover. Let stand 1 hour. Drain beans; return
pan. Add broth; bring to a boil. Cover, reduce
t, and simmer 1 hour or until tender. Remove
cup cooked beans with a slotted spoon; mash
h a fork. Return mashed beans to pan; set aside.
Coat a nonstick skillet with cooking spray; add
and place over medium-high heat until hot.
d onion, sliced green onions, and garlic; sauté

until tender. Add chicken; cook until browned,
stirring to crumble. Add chicken mixture, corn,
and next 4 ingredients to bean mixture in pan;
bring to a boil. Reduce heat, and simmer, uncovered, 20 minutes. Sprinkle cornmeal over chili;
cook until thick, stirring frequently. Ladle into
bowls; top with chopped green onions, if desired.
Yield: 4 servings (serving size: 1½ cups).

Selections: 3 P/M, 1 FA, 1 FR/V, 1 B; **Points:** 3
Per serving: CAL 284 (15% from fat); PRO 26.1g; FAT 4.6g (sat
1.1g); CARB 35.7g; FIB 14.9g; CHOL 53mg; IRON 3.4mg; SOD
512mg; CALC 91mg

Chunky Chicken Noodle Soup

4   cups water
8   (6-ounce) skinned chicken breast halves
¾   teaspoon poultry seasoning
¼   teaspoon dried thyme
3   celery leaves
2   cups water
2   cups uncooked yolk-free egg noodles
½   cup sliced celery
½   cup sliced carrot
⅓   cup sliced green onions
2   tablespoons minced fresh parsley
1½ teaspoons chicken-flavored bouillon granules
½   teaspoon coarsely ground pepper
1   bay leaf
Additional coarsely ground pepper

1. Combine first 5 ingredients in a large Dutch
oven; bring to boil. Cover, reduce heat, and simmer 45 minutes or until chicken is tender.
2. Remove chicken with a slotted spoon; let cool
slightly. Remove bones from chicken, and dis-

Souped Up Broth

If you prefer to make your own chicken broth
or beef broth instead of using canned, here's a
suggestion for adding extra flavor to homemade broths: Pan-roast the meat pieces and
bones first.

Simply broil the meat pieces and bones on the
rack of a broiler pan, turning them occasionally
until browned on all sides. Wipe excess fat
from the pieces by patting dry with a paper
towel, and proceed with your broth recipe.

card. Coarsely chop chicken; set aside. Skim fat from broth; strain broth through a double layer of cheesecloth. Discard solids.

3. Combine broth, 2 cups water, and next 8 ingredients in pan. Bring to a boil; cover. Reduce heat; simmer 20 minutes, stirring occasionally. Add chicken; bring to a boil. Reduce heat; simmer 5 minutes, stirring occasionally. Discard bay leaf. Sprinkle each serving with additional pepper, if desired. Yield: 12 servings (serving size: 1 cup).

Selections: 2 P/M, 50 C; **Points:** 3
Per serving: CAL 145 (19% from fat); PRO 20.9g; FAT 3.1g (sat 0.7g); CARB 6.7g; FIB 0.3g; CHOL 52mg; IRON 0.8mg; SOD 193mg; CALC 16mg

Fresh Tomato Soup With Basil

Cooking spray
4½ cups chopped seeded peeled tomato
¾ cup chopped onion
½ cup chopped celery
1 cup water
1 teaspoon chicken-flavored bouillon granules
½ teaspoon sugar
¼ teaspoon freshly ground pepper
⅓ cup finely chopped fresh basil
Basil sprigs (optional)

1. Coat a Dutch oven with cooking spray; place over medium heat until hot. Add tomato, onion and celery; sauté 5 minutes or until onion is tender. Add water, bouillon granules, sugar, and pepper; bring to boil. Cover, reduce heat, and simmer 30 minutes, stirring occasionally.

2. Pour half of tomato mixture into a blender or food processor; process until smooth. Pour into a bowl. Repeat procedure with remaining tomato mixture. Stir in chopped basil; cover and chill. Garnish each serving with basil sprigs, if desired. Yield: 5 servings (serving size: 1 cup).

Selections: 1 FR/V; **Points:** 0.5
Per serving: CAL 55 (16% from fat); PRO 2.1g; FAT 1g (sat 0.1g); CARB 11.7g; FIB 3.1; CHOL 0mg; IRON 1mg; SOD 191mg; CALC 23mg

Easy Sausage Chili

¾ pound bulk turkey sausage
1 cup chopped onion

1 cup chopped green bell pepper
1 cup chopped celery
¼ cup no-salt-added tomato paste
½ teaspoon dried thyme
¼ teaspoon pepper
2 (14½-ounce) cans no-salt-added whole tomatoes, undrained and chopped
1 (15-ounce) can no-salt-added kidney beans, drained
¼ cup fat-free sour cream
Diced tomato (optional)
Thyme sprigs (optional)

1. Combine sausage, onion, bell pepper, a celery in a large Dutch oven; cook over mediu heat until sausage is browned and vegetables tender, stirring to crumble sausage. Drain m ture in a colander. Wipe drippings from pan wi a paper towel.

2. Return sausage mixture to pan. Add toma paste and next 4 ingredients; bring to a bc Cover, reduce heat, and simmer 35 minutes, st ring occasionally.

3. Ladle chili into bowls; top with sour crea Garnish with diced tomato and thyme sprigs, desired. Yield: 4 servings (serving size: 1½ cu chili and 1 tablespoon sour cream).

Selections: 3 P/M, 2 FR/V, 50 C; **Points:** 6
Per serving: CAL 304 (28% from fat); PRO 23.4g; FAT 9.3g (2.6g); CARB 34.4g; FIB 6.4g; CHOL 52mg; IRON 5mg; S 528mg; CALC 161mg

Chunky Gazpacho

2¼ cups coarsely chopped peeled tomato
1½ cups no-salt-added tomato juice
¾ cup diced seeded peeled cucumber
3 tablespoons chopped fresh parsley
2 tablespoons chopped onion
1 tablespoon balsamic vinegar
½ teaspoon ground cumin
½ teaspoon minced jalapeño pepper
⅛ teaspoon salt
⅛ teaspoon coarsely ground pepper
1 small garlic clove, minced
Sliced green onions (optional)

1. Combine first 11 ingredients in a blender, a process until mixture is chunky. Pour into a bov cover and chill.

Sausage Chili

Black-eyed Pea Gumbo

Ladle soup into individual bowls. Garnish with sliced green onions, if desired. Yield: 4 servings (serving size: 1 cup).

Selections: 1 FR/V; Points: 0.5
Per serving: CAL 46 (8% from fat); PRO 2.1g; FAT 0.4g (sat 0.1g); CARB 10.7g; FIB 1.9g; CHOL 0mg; IRON 1.43mg; SOD 96mg; CALC 26.5mg

Black-eyed Pea Gumbo

   (¾-pound) pork tenderloin
Cooking spray
   (15-ounce) cans black-eyed peas, undrained
   (14¼-ounce) can fat-free beef broth
   (16-ounce) package frozen vegetable
   gumbo mix
   tablespoon dried parsley flakes
   teaspoons hot sauce
   teaspoon dried thyme
   teaspoon ground red pepper
   garlic cloves, minced
   bay leaves
½ cups hot cooked long-grain rice

Trim fat from pork; cut pork into bite-size pieces. Coat a Dutch oven with cooking spray; place over medium heat until hot. Add pork; sauté until browned. Stir in peas and next 8 ingredients; bring to a boil. Reduce heat, and simmer, uncovered, 20 minutes. Discard bay leaves.

Spoon rice into individual bowls, and top with gumbo. Yield: 5 servings (serving size: ½ cup rice and 1½ cups gumbo).

Selections: 2 P/M, 1 B, 1 FR/V, 80 C; Points: 8
Per serving: CAL 424 (7% from fat); PRO 31.6g; FAT 3.3g (sat 1g); CARB 65.8g; FIB 6g; CHOL 44mg; IRON 4.5mg; SOD 594mg; CALC 78mg

Baked Potato Soup With Bacon

   pound baking potatoes, cubed
   cups 2% low-fat milk
   teaspoons reduced-calorie stick margarine
   teaspoon salt
   teaspoon pepper
   cup sliced green onions
   teaspoons bottled real bacon bits

Place potatoes in a medium saucepan. Cover with water, and bring to a boil. Cook 15 minutes or until very tender, and drain. Return potatoes

to pan, and mash to desired consistency. Add milk, margarine, salt, and pepper, and stir well. Cook over medium heat until thoroughly heated, stirring frequently.

2. Ladle soup into individual bowls; top with green onions and bacon bits. Yield: 2 servings (serving size: 2 cups soup, 2 tablespoons green onions, and 2 teaspoons bacon bits).

Selections: 2 B, 1 P/M, 1 FA, 30 C; Points: 7
Per serving: CAL 364 (21% from fat); PRO 14.6g; FAT 8.4g (sat 3.4g); CARB 58.4g; FIB 3.8g; CHOL 23mg; IRON 1.1mg; SOD 922mg; CALC 320mg

Chilled Cucumber Soup

½ cup plain fat-free yogurt
1 tablespoon reduced-calorie stick margarine
Cooking spray
1 cup chopped seeded peeled cucumber
2 tablespoons chopped green onions
2 teaspoons cornstarch
1¼ cups skim milk, divided
½ teaspoon chicken-flavored bouillon
   granules
¼ teaspoon dried dill
Thin cucumber slices (optional)
Chopped green onions (optional)

1. Spoon yogurt onto several layers of heavy-duty paper towels; spread to ½-inch thickness. Cover with additional paper towels; let stand 5 minutes. Scrape into a medium bowl, using a rubber spatula; set aside.

2. Melt margarine in a small saucepan coated with cooking spray over medium heat. Add cucumber

Baked Potato Soup With Bacon and Roasted Vegetable Pitas With Sour Cream (page 31).

and green onions; sauté until tender. Combine cornstarch and ¼ cup milk; stir well. Add cornstarch mixture, remaining 1 cup milk, bouillon granules, and dill to pan; bring to a boil, stirring constantly. Reduce heat; simmer 1 minute, stirring constantly. Remove from heat; let cool slightly.

3. Pour cucumber mixture into a blender; process until smooth. Gradually stir puréed cucumber mixture into yogurt; cover and chill.

4. Ladle soup into bowls. Garnish with cucumber slices and green onions, if desired. Yield: 2 servings (serving size: 1 cup).

Selections: 1 P/M, 1 FA, 1 FR/V; **Points:** 3
Per serving: CAL 139 (28% from fat); PRO 9.1g; FAT 4.4g (sat 0.9g); CARB 16.8g; FIB 0.9g; CHOL 0mg; IRON 0.4mg; SOD 96mg; CALC 317mg

Quick-and-Easy Vegetable Soup

1 pound ultra-lean ground beef
1¼ cups chopped onion
8 (5.5-ounce) cans low-sodium vegetable juice
2 (14½-ounce) cans no-salt-added whole tomatoes, undrained and coarsely chopped
1 (14¼-ounce) can fat-free beef broth
1 (10-ounce) package frozen sliced okra
1 (10-ounce) package frozen baby lima beans
1 (10-ounce) package frozen whole-kernel corn
1 teaspoon coarsely ground pepper
½ teaspoon salt

1. Cook beef and onion in a Dutch oven over medium-high heat until beef is browned, stirring to crumble. Drain in a colander. Wipe drippings from pan with a paper towel.

2. Return beef mixture to pan. Stir in vegetable juice and remaining ingredients. Bring to a boil; cover, reduce heat, and simmer 1 hour. Yield: 12 servings (serving size: 1½ cups).

Selections: 1 P/M, 1 FR/V, 30 C; **Points:** 3
Per serving: CAL 143 (16% from fat); PRO 11.1g; FAT 2.6g (sat 0.9g); CARB 21g; FIB 2g; CHOL 22mg; IRON 2.5mg; SOD 238mg; CALC 70mg

Simple Minestrone

2 cups diced zucchini
½ cup uncooked ditalini (small tubular-shaped pasta)

⅛ teaspoon pepper
2 garlic cloves, minced
2 (16-ounce) cans one-third-less salt chicken broth
1 (14½-ounce) can Italian-style stewed tomatoes, undrained and coarsely chopped
1 (16-ounce) can red kidney beans, drained
1 (10-ounce) package frozen peas and carrots, thawed
½ cup grated Parmesan cheese

1. Combine first 8 ingredients in a large saucepan; bring to a boil. Cover, reduce heat, and simmer 10 minutes or until pasta is done, stirring occasionally. Stir in cheese. Yield: 9 servings (serving size: 1 cup).

Selections: 1 FR/V, 1 P/M; **Points:** 3
Per serving: CAL 138 (13% from fat); PRO 8.9g; FAT 2g (sat 1g); CARB 20.5g; FIB 1.6g; CHOL 4mg; IRON 2mg; SOD 324mg; CALC 98mg

Cream of Broccoli Soup

1 (10-ounce) package frozen chopped broccoli
2 tablespoons reduced-calorie stick margarine
Cooking spray
⅔ cup sliced mushrooms
⅔ cup chopped onion
3 tablespoons all-purpose flour
¾ cup fat-free chicken broth
1 (12-ounce) can evaporated skim milk
½ teaspoon salt
¼ teaspoon dried thyme
¼ teaspoon pepper

1. Cook broccoli according to package directions; drain well, and set aside.

2. Melt margarine in a large saucepan coated with cooking spray over medium heat. Add mushrooms and onion; sauté until tender. Add flour; cook 1 minute, stirring constantly. Gradually add chicken broth and milk; cook until mixture is thick and bubbly, stirring constantly. Add broccoli, salt, thyme, and pepper; cook until mixture is thoroughly heated, stirring frequently. Yield: 4 servings (serving size: 1 cup).

Selections: 1 FR/V, 1 FA, 1 P/M; **Points:** 3
Per serving: CAL 155 (27% from fat); PRO 10g; FAT 4.6g (sat 0.8g); CARB 20.2g; FIB 2.7g; CHOL 3mg; IRON 1.5mg; SOD 489mg; CALC 295mg

Simple Minestrone goes together in minutes with canned and frozen vegetables.

In the Mood for Something Sweet

SATISFY YOUR DESSERT DESIRES SENSIBLY
WITH OUR SUGARY NOTIONS.

*I*f *you think the differences between men and women stop at muscles and mothering, you're wrong. It gets much more nitpicky than that—even down to our choices in cravings. Women opt for foods that meet needs other than their health (emotional eating, if you will). More than half of all women nosh to relax, and about as many reach for sweets when they are depressed. In fact, two of the top three sources of carbohydrates in the typical American woman's diet are sugar and soft drinks. But ask a man what he snacks on and he is likely to tell you something savory or salty. And if you ask him about a food he yearns for, he probably will say something like a steak, spaghetti, or seafood. Women call those entrées.*

Regardless of gender or emotional disposition, most of us would find it hard to resist a plate of piping-hot Peach Cobbler or a crispy little Snickerdoodle. That's doubly true if you know that the recipes are streamlined to fit into a sensible eating philosophy and a busy life—just like the ones found on the following pages.

A low-fat dough flavored with peach syrup bakes up around peach slices for a healthy Peach Cobbler.

Peach Cobbler

Cooking spray
¼ cup reduced-calorie stick margarine, melted
2 (16-ounce) cans sliced peaches in light syrup, undrained
¾ cup all-purpose flour
⅔ cup sugar
1 teaspoon baking powder
¼ cup skim milk

1. Preheat oven to 375°.

2. Coat a 9-inch square baking dish with cooking spray; add melted margarine, and set aside. Drain peaches, reserving ½ cup syrup, and set aside.

3. Combine flour, sugar, and baking powder in a medium bowl. Add the reserved syrup and skim milk to dry ingredients, stirring just until moist.

4. Pour batter into prepared dish, and top with peaches (do not stir). Bake at 375° for 35 minutes or until golden. Yield: 6 servings.

Selections: 1 FA, 1 FR/V, 1 B, 70C; **Points:** 5
Per serving: CAL 244 (19% from fat); PRO 2.5g; FAT 5.2g (sat 0.7g); CARB 50g; FIB 0.8g; CHOL 0mg; IRON 1.2mg; SOD 85mg; CALC 64mg

Enjoy Caramel-Baked Pears topped with almonds as a light ending to your evening meal.

Caramel-Baked Pears

⅓ cup firmly packed brown sugar
¼ cup water
2 teaspoons margarine
2 medium firm ripe pears (about 1 pound)
2 tablespoons vanilla low-fat yogurt
2 teaspoons sliced almonds, toasted

1. Preheat oven to 350°.

2. Combine first 3 ingredients in a small saucepan. Bring to a boil, and cook 3 minutes or until slightly thick. Remove pan from heat; set caramel mixture aside.

3. Peel and core pears; cut pears in half lengthwise. Arrange pear halves, cut sides up, in an 8-inch square baking dish; drizzle caramel mixture over pears. Cover and bake at 350° for 25 minutes. Uncover and bake an additional 25 minutes or until tender.

4. Place 2 pear halves in each of 2 dessert dishes. spoon caramel mixture evenly over pears. Top each serving with 1 tablespoon yogurt and 1 teaspoon almonds. Yield: 2 servings.

Selections: 1 FR/V, 1 FA, 150 C; **Points:** 5
Per serving: CAL 291 (18% from fat); PRO 1.8g; FAT 5.7g (sat 1g); CARB 62.7g; FIB 4.5g; CHOL 1mg; IRON 1.2mg; SOD 68mg; CALC 80mg

Snickerdoodles

1½ cups sugar
¾ cup reduced-calorie stick margarine, softened
1 teaspoon vanilla extract
2 large eggs
4 cups all-purpose flour
2 teaspoons cream of tartar
1 teaspoon baking soda
½ teaspoon salt
2 tablespoons sugar
1½ teaspoons ground cinnamon
Cooking spray

1. Combine 1½ cups sugar and margarine; beat at medium speed of a mixer until light and fluffy. Add vanilla and eggs; beat well. Combine flour and next 3 ingredients; add to creamed mixture, beating well. Cover and chill 2 hours.

2. Preheat oven to 400°.

Combine 2 tablespoons sugar and cinnamon
 small bowl; stir well, and set aside.

Shape dough into 1-inch balls; roll in sugar
xture. Place 2 inches apart on a baking sheet
ted with cooking spray. Bake at 400° for 8
nutes or until lightly browned. Let cool on
 1 minute; remove from pan. Let cool com-
tely on wire racks. Yield: 6 dozen (serving
: 1 cookie).

ctions: 60 C; **Points:** 1
 serving: CAL 55 (23% from fat); PRO 0.9g; FAT 1.4g (sat 0.2g);
B 9.9g; FIB 0.2g; CHOL 6mg; IRON 0.3mg; SOD 54mg; CALC

ple-Oat Crumble

 cups sliced peeled Granny Smith apples
 teaspoon grated orange rind
 cup fresh orange juice
 cup sugar
 cup regular oats
 cup all-purpose flour
 teaspoon ground cinnamon
 teaspoon ground nutmeg
 teaspoon salt
 tablespoons chilled reduced-calorie stick
  margarine, cut into small pieces
 tablespoons frozen reduced-calorie
  whipped topping, thawed

Preheat oven to 375°.

Place apple slices in an 8-inch square baking
, and sprinkle with orange rind and juice.

Combine sugar and next 5 ingredients in a
wl; stir well. Cut in margarine with a pastry
nder or 2 knives until mixture resembles
rse meal. Sprinkle mixture over apple slices.
ke at 375° for 40 minutes or until apples are
der and topping is lightly browned. Top each
ving with 1 tablespoon whipped topping.
ld: 6 servings.

ections: 1 FR/V, 120 C; **Points:** 3.5
 serving: CAL 171 (25% from fat); PRO 1.6g; FAT 4.7g (sat
); CARB 32.6g; FIB 1.8g; CHOL 0mg; IRON 0.6mg; SOD
mg; CALC 12mg

tterscotch Brownies

 tablespoons stick margarine, softened
 cups firmly packed dark brown sugar

½ cup egg substitute
2   teaspoons vanilla extract
2   cups all-purpose flour
1   teaspoon baking powder
¼   teaspoon baking soda
½   teaspoon salt
⅔   cup butterscotch chips
Cooking spray

1. Preheat oven to 350°.

2. Combine margarine and sugar in a bowl; beat
at medium speed of a mixer until light and
fluffy. Add egg substitute and vanilla extract,
and beat well.

3. Combine flour, baking powder, baking soda,
and salt. Add to creamed mixture; beat well. Stir
in butterscotch chips.

4. Spoon mixture into a 13- x 9-inch baking pan
coated with cooking spray. Bake at 350° for 25
minutes or until a wooden pick inserted in center
comes out clean. Let cool completely on a wire
rack. Yield: 2½ dozen (serving size: 1 brownie).

Selections: 1 FA, 70 C; **Points:** 2.5
Per serving: CAL 115 (26% from fat); PRO 1.4g; FAT 3.3g (sat
0.6g); CARB 19.8g; FIB 0.2g; CHOL 0mg; IRON 0.7mg; SOD
89mg; CALC 27mg

**Apple-Oat Crumble is a
British dessert that gets
its name from the
crumbly pastry topping.**

MILKING FAT OUT OF YOUR DIET

If you're trying to cut back on fat, don't forget milk. Consider that whole milk, which may be labeled as containing only 3.5% to 3.7% fat by weight, actually gets more than 50% of its calories from fat. (In fact, whole milk ranks as the second largest contributor of saturated fat to the American diet—the hamburger is number one.)

Think 2% milk is the lean alternative? Wrong. This milk still contains about five grams of fat per 8-ounce serving. Part of the problem is that manufacturers homogenize, or blend, the cream back into the whole and low-fat milks. Only skim (non-fat) milk is free from this added fat. For a low-fat diet, choose at least 1% low-fat milk or, preferably, skim milk.

Peach Ice Cream

5   cups chopped peeled ripe fresh peaches (about 3 pounds), divided
⅔   cup sugar
1   tablespoon lemon juice
2   cups 2% reduced-fat milk
1   cup evaporated skim milk
½   cup egg substitute
2   tablespoons honey
⅛   teaspoon almond extract
Mint sprigs (optional)

1. Mash 4 cups peaches in a large bowl. Add sugar and lemon juice; stir well. Let stand 30 minutes, stirring occasionally. Add milks, egg substitute, honey, and extract; beat at medium speed of a mixer until well blended. Stir in remaining 1 cup peaches.

2. Pour mixture into freezer can of an ice cream freezer; freeze according to manufacturer's instructions. Spoon ice cream into a freezer-safe container; cover and freeze 1 hour or until firm. Garnish with mint sprigs, if desired. Yield: 20 servings (serving size: ½ cup).

Selections: 50 C; **Points:** 1
Per serving: CAL 77 (6% from fat); PRO 2.7g; FAT 0.5g (sat 0.3g); CARB 16.3g; FIB 0.7g; CHOL 2mg; IRON 0.2mg; SOD 36mg; CALC 71mg

Chocolate-Mint Ice Cream

½   cup sugar
¼   cup nonfat dry milk powder
¼   cup unsweetened cocoa
2   tablespoons cornstarch
2   cups 1% low-fat milk
1   (12-ounce) can evaporated skim milk
1   large egg yolk, lightly beaten
2   teaspoons vanilla extract
¼   teaspoon peppermint extract

1. Combine first 4 ingredients in a medium saucepan, and stir well. Gradually add milks, stirring with a whisk until blended. Cook over medium heat until slightly thick, stirring constantly. Gradually stir about one-fourth of hot mixture into egg yolk, and add to remaining hot mixture, stirring constantly. Cook over low heat 1 minute or until mixture is thick, stirring constantly. Remove from heat, and stir in extracts.

Peach Ice Cream

Pour into a bowl, and cover surface of pudding with plastic wrap; chill.

2. Pour mixture into freezer can of an ice cream freezer; freeze according to manufacturer's instructions. Spoon ice cream into a freezer-safe container; cover and freeze 1 hour or until firm. Yield: 7 servings (serving size: ½ cup).

Selections: 1 P/M, 70 C; **Points:** 4
Per serving: CAL 174 (10% from fat); PRO 8.8g; FAT 2g (sat 1g); CARB 29.4g; FIB 0g; CHOL 37mg; IRON 0.8mg; SOD 116mg; CALC 289mg

Almond-Mocha Parfaits

1½ cups vanilla low-fat ice cream
1   teaspoon instant espresso granules
4   teaspoons amaretto
¼   cup chocolate wafer crumbs (about 4 cookies)
2   tablespoons frozen reduced-calorie whipped topping, thawed
2   whole coffee beans (optional)

1. Combine vanilla ice cream and instant espresso granules, and stir well.

2. Spoon ¼ cup ice cream mixture into each of 2 (8-ounce) parfait glasses; top ice cream mixture with 1 teaspoon amaretto and 1 tablespoon chocolate wafer crumbs. Repeat layers, ending with ice cream mixture; freeze 1 hour. To serve, top each parfait with 1 tablespoon whipped topping. Garnish each serving with a whole coffee bean, if desired. Serve immediately. Yield: 2 servings.

Selections: 230 C; **Points:** 5
Per serving: CAL 229 (28% from fat); PRO 4.8g; FAT 7.2g (sat 3.6g); CARB 32g; FIB 0g; CHOL 23mg; IRON 0.4mg; SOD 126mg; CALC 149mg

Vanilla Pudding

½   cup sugar
2½ tablespoons cornstarch
⅛   teaspoon salt
2   cups skim milk
1   large egg, lightly beaten
1   tablespoon reduced-calorie stick margarine
2   teaspoons vanilla extract
Edible snapdragons (optional)

1. Combine first 3 ingredients in a saucepan. Add milk and egg; stir with a whisk until well blended.

Place over medium heat, and bring to a boil, stirring constantly.

2. Remove from heat; stir in margarine and vanilla. Divide pudding evenly among 4 (6-ounce) custard cups. Cover surface of each pudding with plastic wrap; chill at least 45 minutes. Garnish with snapdragons, if desired. Yield: 4 servings.

Selections: 1 P/M, 1 FA, 70 C; **Points:** 4
Per serving: CAL 201 (15% from fat); PRO 5.8g; FAT 3.3g (sat 0.8g); CARB 36.4g; FIB 0g; CHOL 58mg; IRON 0.3mg; SOD 182mg; CALC 158mg

Carrot-Raisin Snack Cake

½ cup firmly packed dark brown sugar
⅓ cup stick margarine, softened
⅔ cup unsweetened applesauce
½ cup egg substitute
1½ cups sifted cake flour
1½ teaspoons baking powder
1 teaspoon ground cinnamon
¼ teaspoon salt
1 cup finely shredded carrot
½ cup raisins
Cooking spray
1 tablespoon powdered sugar

1. Preheat oven to 350°.

2. Combine brown sugar and margarine; beat at medium speed of a mixer until light and fluffy. Add applesauce and egg substitute; beat well. Combine flour and next 3 ingredients; add to creamed mixture, stirring well. Stir in carrot and raisins.

3. Pour batter into an 8-inch square baking pan coated with cooking spray. Bake at 350° for 25 minutes or until a wooden pick inserted in center comes out clean. Let cake cool in pan on a wire rack. Sift powdered sugar over cooled cake. Yield: 9 servings.

Selections: 1 B, 1 FA, 1 FR/V, 40 C; **Points:** 5
Per serving: CAL 218 (29% from fat); PRO 3.3g; FAT 7g (sat 1.4g); CARB 36.6g; FIB 1g; CHOL 0mg; IRON 2.2mg; SOD 174mg; CALC 75mg

Orange Pound Cake Loaf

Cooking spray
1 teaspoon all-purpose flour
1¾ cups all-purpose flour
¾ cup sugar
2 teaspoons baking powder

¼ teaspoon salt
1 tablespoon grated orange rind
⅔ cup fresh orange juice
¼ cup vegetable oil
4 large egg whites

1. Preheat oven to 350°.

2. Coat bottom of an 8½- x 4½-inch loaf pan with cooking spray; dust with 1 teaspoon flour and set aside.

3. Combine 1¾ cups flour, sugar, baking powder, and salt. Combine orange rind, juice, and oil; add to flour mixture. Beat at medium speed of mixer until smooth (batter will be thick).

Beat egg whites at high speed of a mixer until [st]iff peaks form. Fold one third of egg whites into [ba]tter; gently fold in remaining egg whites.

Pour batter into prepared pan. Bake at 350° for [...] minutes or until a wooden pick inserted in [ce]nter comes out clean. Let cake cool in pan 10 [mi]nutes on a wire rack; remove from pan. Let [co]ol completely on wire rack. Yield: 16 servings [(se]rving size: 1 slice).

[S]ections: 1 B, 1 FA; **Points:** 3
[Pe]r **serving:** CAL 126 (26% from fat); PRO 2.4g; FAT 3.6g (sat [...]g); CARB 21.3g; FIB 0.4g; CHOL 0mg; IRON 0.7mg; SOD [...]mg; CALC 26mg

Individual Caramel Custards

2   tablespoons sugar
Cooking spray
2½ cups skim milk
1   cup egg substitute
⅓   cup sugar
1¼ teaspoons vanilla extract

1. Preheat oven to 300°.

2. Place 2 tablespoons sugar in a small heavy saucepan over medium heat; cook until sugar dissolves, stirring constantly. Continue cooking an additional 5 minutes or until golden, stirring frequently. Immediately pour into 6 (6-ounce) cus-

This Orange Pound Cake Loaf is proof that healthy desserts can satisfy a sweet tooth without sacrificing flavor.

Ginger Cookies

tard cups coated with cooking spray, tipping quickly until caramelized sugar coats bottom of cups; set aside (caramel syrup will harden).

3. Combine milk and next 3 ingredients; stir well with a whisk. Divide evenly among custard cups. Place cups in a 13- x 9-inch baking pan; pour hot water into pan to a depth of 1 inch. Bake at 300° for 1 hour and 10 minutes or until a knife inserted in center comes out clean. Remove cups from water; let cool completely. Cover; chill at least 2 hours.

4. Loosen edges of custards with a knife or rubber spatula. Invert custard cups onto individual plates. Yield: 6 servings.

Selections: 1 P/M, 60 C; **Points:** 2
Per serving: CAL 120 (3% from fat); PRO 7.5g; FAT 0.4g (sat 0.1g); CARB 21.1g; FIB 0g; CHOL 2mg; IRON 0.8mg; SOD 113mg; CALC 139mg

Ginger Cookies

6   tablespoons stick margarine, softened
⅔   cup sugar
¼   cup molasses
1   large egg
2   cups all-purpose flour
2   teaspoons baking soda
1   teaspoon ground ginger
1   teaspoon ground cinnamon
½   teaspoon ground mace
3   tablespoons sugar
Cooking spray

1. Cream margarine; gradually add ⅔ cup sugar, beating at medium speed of a mixer until light and fluffy. Add molasses and egg, and beat well.

2. Combine flour and next 4 ingredients; gradually add to creamed mixture, stirring until well blended. Divide dough in half; wrap each portion in plastic wrap, and freeze for 30 minutes.

3. Preheat oven to 350°.

4. Shape each portion of dough into 26 (1-inch) balls; roll in remaining 3 tablespoons sugar. Place balls 2 inches apart on baking sheets coated with cooking spray. Bake at 350° for 12 minutes or until lightly browned. Remove from baking sheets; let cool completely on wire racks. Store in an airtight container. Yield: 52 cookies (serving size: 1 cookie).

Selections: 50 C; **Points:** 1
Per serving: CAL 46 (29% from fat); PRO 0.6g; FAT 1.5g (sat 0.3g); CARB 7.7g; FIB 0.1g; CHOL 4mg; IRON 0.3mg; SOD 49mg; CALC 13mg

Banana Pudding

2½   tablespoons sugar
2½   teaspoons cornstarch
Dash of salt
¾   cup skim milk
1   large egg yolk
½   cup sliced ripe banana
¼   teaspoon vanilla extract
8   vanilla wafers

1. Combine first 3 ingredients in top of a double boiler. Gradually add milk and egg yolk, stirring constantly with a whisk until blended. Place over simmering water; cook 4 minutes or until smooth and thick, stirring constantly. Remove from heat; stir in banana and vanilla.

2. Divide mixture evenly between 2 (6-ounce) custard cups. Arrange 4 cookies around edge of each cup, pushing cookies into pudding. Cover with plastic wrap; chill at least 2 hours. Yield: 2 servings.

Selections: 210 C; **Points:** 5
Per serving: CAL 248 (23% from fat); PRO 5.7g; FAT 6.4g (sat 2.4g); CARB 42.3g; FIB 1.1g; CHOL 111mg; IRON 0.8mg; SOD 264mg; CALC 134mg

Black Forest Trifle

6   tablespoons sugar
¼   cup unsweetened cocoa
3½   tablespoons cornstarch
2   cups 1% low-fat milk
1   tablespoon margarine

Banana Pudding

¾ teaspoon vanilla extract
1 (15-ounce) loaf fat-free chocolate
   pound cake
¼ cup kirsch (cherry-flavored liqueur)
1 (20-ounce) can light cherry pie filling
2 cups frozen reduced-calorie whipped
   topping, thawed
Fresh cherries (optional)
Chocolate curls (optional)

1. Combine cocoa, cornstarch, and milk in a saucepan. Gradually add milk, stirring with a whisk until blended. Cook over medium heat for 5 minutes until mixture is thick, stirring constantly. Remove from heat. Add margarine and vanilla, stirring until margarine melts. Pour into a bowl, and cover surface of pudding with plastic wrap; chill.

2. Cut pound cake into 1-inch cubes. Arrange half of cake cubes in a 3-quart trifle bowl, and brush with 2 tablespoons liqueur. Spoon half of cherry pie filling over cake cubes. Spread half of chocolate pudding over cherry pie filling. Top with half of whipped topping. Repeat layers with remaining cake cubes, liqueur, cherry pie filling, chocolate pudding, and whipped topping. Cover and refrigerate at least 8 hours. Garnish with fresh cherries and chocolate curls, if desired. Yield: 12 servings.

Selections: 230 C; **Points:** 5
Per serving: CAL 234 (12% from fat); PRO 3.9g; FAT 3g (sat 1.6g); CARB 41.3g; FIB 1.4g; CHOL 2mg; IRON 1mg; SOD 220mg; CALC 68mg

Desserts are one of life's simple pleasures, so go ahead and treat yourself to Black Forest Trifle or Cinnamon-Crusted Baked Apples.

Cinnamon-Crusted Baked Apples

Butter-flavored cooking spray
⅓ cup water
5 medium cooking apples, peeled, cored, and cut into ½-inch wedges
⅓ cup firmly packed brown sugar
¼ cup all-purpose flour
½ teaspoon ground cinnamon
¼ teaspoon ground nutmeg
2 tablespoons chilled reduced-calorie stick margarine, cut into small pieces

1. Preheat oven to 350°.

2. Coat an 11- x 7-inch baking dish with cooking spray, and pour water into dish. Arrange apples in prepared dish, and lightly coat apples with cooking spray.

3. Combine brown sugar, flour, cinnamon, and nutmeg; cut in margarine with a pastry blender or 2 knives until mixture resembles coarse meal. Sprinkle mixture evenly over apples. Bake at 350° for 30 minutes or until apples are tender. Yield: 8 servings.

Selections: 1 B, 1 FA; **Points:** 2
Per serving: CAL 127 (16% from fat); PRO 0.5g; FAT 2.3g (sa 0.3g); CARB 28.4g; FIB 3.2g; CHOL 0mg; IRON 0.4mg; SOD 30mg; CALC 15mg

Pineapple Upside-Down Cake

1 small pineapple, peeled and cored
6 tablespoons dark brown sugar
1 tablespoon stick margarine
¼ cup pineapple juice
2 tablespoons finely chopped walnuts

cup egg substitute
cup sugar
tablespoons stick margarine, melted
½ cups sifted cake flour
teaspoons baking powder
teaspoon salt
cup skim milk
teaspoons vanilla extract

Preheat oven to 350°.

Cut pineapple crosswise into 4 (½-inch-ick) slices. Cut 3 pineapple slices in half, and slices aside. Reserve remaining pineapple for other use.

Combine brown sugar and 1 tablespoon mar-garine in an 8-inch cast iron skillet; cook over medium heat 1 minute. Add pineapple juice, and cook 1 minute, stirring constantly. Remove from heat; sprinkle chopped walnuts over sugar mix-ture. Place whole pineapple slice in center of skil-let. Arrange halved pineapple slices around center slice, and set aside.

4. Beat egg substitute at high speed of a mixer until foamy. Add ½ cup sugar and melted margarine, and beat mixture well. Combine sifted cake flour, baking powder, and salt, and stir well. Add flour mixture to egg substitute

Chopped walnuts, thick slices of fresh pineapple, and caramelized sugar top Pineapple Upside-Down Cake.

mixture alternately with skim milk, beginning and ending with flour mixture; beat well after each addition. Stir in vanilla extract, and pour batter over pineapple slices. Bake at 350° for 45 minutes or until a wooden pick inserted in center comes out clean. Let cake cool in skillet 5 minutes, and invert onto a serving plate. Yield: 10 servings.

Selections: 1 FR/V, 1 FA, 1 B, 50 C; **Points:** 4
Per serving: CAL 182 (23% from fat); PRO 2.7g; FAT 4.6g (sat 0.7g); CARB 32.9g; FIB 1.1g; CHOL 0mg; IRON 1.7mg; SOD 177mg; CALC 84mg

Lemon Cream Pie

1   cup low-fat cinnamon crisp graham cracker crumbs (about 7 crackers)
¼   cup reduced-calorie stick margarine, melted
¾   cup sugar
7   tablespoons cornstarch
⅛   teaspoon salt
1   cup water
⅔   cup low-fat buttermilk
½   cup egg substitute
2   teaspoons grated lemon rind
½   cup fresh lemon juice
2½ cups frozen reduced-calorie whipped topping, thawed
Lemon zest (optional)
Lemon rind curls (optional)
Lemon slices (optional)
Mint sprigs (optional)

1. Preheat oven to 350°.
2. Combine graham cracker crumbs and ma garine; stir well. Press into bottom and up sid of a 9-inch pie plate. Bake at 350° for 8 mi utes or until golden. Let cool completely on wire rack.
3. Combine sugar, cornstarch, and salt in saucepan, and gradually stir in water and lo fat buttermilk. Bring to a boil over mediu heat, and cook 1 minute or until thick, stirri constantly.
4. Gradually stir about one-fourth of the h mixture into egg substitute, and add to the r maining hot mixture, stirring constantly. Co over medium heat 2 minutes or until thic stirring constantly. Remove from heat, and s in 2 teaspoons grated lemon rind and fre lemon juice.
5. Spoon lemon mixture into prepared cru Cover surface of pie with plastic wrap; chi Spread whipped topping over filling just befo serving. Garnish with lemon zest, lemon ri curls, lemon slices, and mint, if desired. Yie 8 servings.

Selections: 1 FA, 180 C; **Points:** 5.5
Per serving: CAL 251 (26% from fat); PRO 4.1g; FAT 7.2g (2.6g); CARB 46.4g; FIB 0.6g; CHOL 1mg; IRON 0.8mg; S 175mg; CALC 47mg

STEP BY STEP WITH CITRUS

Few foods provide the flavor magic of citrus, which adds an unmistakable freshness to a variety of recipes.

Our Lemon Cream Pie relies on lemon juice and grated rind for its tartness. Garnishes of lemon zest, rind curls, and slices hint at the flavor within.

For juicing, gently roll the fruit on a flat surface, using the palm of your hand to soften the pulp.

▼

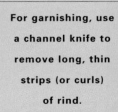

Cut the fruit in half crosswise; then use a hand-held reamer, a citrus juicer, or an electric juicer.

▲

For garnishing, use a channel knife to remove long, thin strips (or curls) of rind.

▼

To obtain the zest, remove only the colored part of the skin with a citrus zester.

▲

INGREDIENT	SUBSTITUTION
BAKING PRODUCTS	
Baking powder, 1 teaspoon	• ½ teaspoon cream of tartar plus ¼ teaspoon baking soda
Chocolate	
semisweet, 1 ounce	• 1 ounce unsweetened chocolate plus 1 tablespoon sugar
unsweetened, 1 ounce or square	• 3 tablespoons cocoa plus 1 tablespoon butter or vegetable shortening
chips, semisweet, 1 ounce	• 1 ounce sweet cooking chocolate
chips, semisweet, 6-ounce package, melted	• 2 ounces unsweetened chocolate, 2 tablespoons vegetable shortening, and ½ cup sugar
Coconut	
flaked, 1 tablespoon	• 1½ tablespoons grated fresh coconut
milk, 1 cup	• 1 cup whole or 2% reduced-fat milk
Corn syrup, light-colored, 1 cup	• 1 cup sugar and ¼ cup water
	• 1 cup honey
Cornstarch, 1 tablespoon (for thickening)	• 2 tablespoons all-purpose flour
	• 2 tablespoons granular tapioca
Cracker crumbs, ¾ cup	• 1 cup dry breadcrumbs
Flour	
all-purpose, 1 tablespoon	• 1½ teaspoons cornstarch, potato starch, or rice starch
	• 1½ tablespoons whole-wheat flour
	• ½ tablespoon whole-wheat flour and ½ tablespoon all-purpose flour
all-purpose, 1 cup sifted	• 1 cup plus 2 tablespoons sifted cake flour
Note: Specialty flours added to	• 1 cup minus 2 tablespoons all-purpose flour (unsifted)
yeast bread will result in a heavier	• 1½ cups breadcrumbs
product with reduced volume.	• 1 cup regular oats
	• ⅓ cup cornmeal or soybean flour and ⅔ cup all-purpose flour
	• ¾ cup whole-wheat flour or bran flour and ¼ cup all-purpose flour
cake, 1 cup sifted	• 1 cup minus 2 tablespoons all-purpose flour
self-rising, 1 cup	• 1 cup all-purpose flour, 1 teaspoon baking powder, and ½ teaspoon salt
Marshmallows, miniature, 1 cup	• 10 large
Pecans, chopped, 1 cup	• 1 cup regular oats, toasted (in baked products)
Sugar	
brown, 1 cup firmly packed	• 1 cup granulated sugar
granulated, 1 teaspoon	• ⅛ teaspoon noncaloric sweetener solution or follow manufacturer's directions
granulated, 1 cup	• 1 cup corn syrup (decrease liquid called for in recipe by ¼ cup)
	• 1⅓ cups molasses (decrease liquid called for in recipe by ⅓ cup)
	• 1 cup firmly packed brown sugar
	• 1 cup honey (decrease liquid called for in recipe by ¼ cup)
powdered, 1 cup	• 1 cup granulated sugar and 1 tablespoon cornstarch (processed in food processor)
Vegetable shortening, melted, 1 cup	• 1 cup cooking oil (cooking oil should not be substituted if recipe does not call for melted shortening)
Vegetable shortening, solid, 1 cup (used in baking)	• 1⅛ cups margarine (decrease salt called for in recipe by ½ teaspoon)
Yeast, dry, 1 tablespoon	• 1 cake yeast, compressed
	• 1 (¼-ounce) package dry yeast
DAIRY PRODUCTS	
Butter, 1 cup	• 1 cup stick margarine
Egg	
1 large	• ¼ cup egg substitute
2 large	• 3 small eggs
white, 1 (2 tablespoons)	• 2 tablespoons egg substitute
	• 2 teaspoons sifted, dry egg white powder and 2 tablespoons warm water
yolk, 1 (1½ tablespoons)	• 2 tablespoons sifted, dry egg yolk powder and 2 teaspoons water
Milk	
low-fat buttermilk, 1 cup	• 1 tablespoon vinegar or lemon juice and skim milk to equal 1 cup (allow to stand 5 to 10 minutes)
	• 1 cup plain low-fat yogurt
	• 1 cup skim milk and 1¾ teaspoons cream of tartar
skim, 1 cup	• 4 to 5 tablespoons nonfat dry milk powder and enough water to make 1 cup, or follow manufacturer's directions
	• ½ cup evaporated skim milk and ½ cup water
fat-free sweetened, condensed, 1 cup	• Add 1 cup plus 2 tablespoons non-fat dry milk powder to ½ cup warm water. Stir well. Add ¾ cup sugar, and stir until smooth.

INGREDIENT	SUBSTITUTION
Sour cream, fat-free, 1 cup	• 1 cup plain fat-free yogurt and 1 tablespoon cornstarch
Yogurt, plain low-fat, 1 cup	• 1 tablespoon lemon juice and evaporated skim milk to equal 1 cup • 1 cup low-fat buttermilk

FRUIT & VEGETABLE PRODUCTS

INGREDIENT	SUBSTITUTION

Lemon
  1 medium
  juice, 1 teaspoon
	• 2 to 3 tablespoons juice and 1 to 2 teaspoons grated rind
	• ½ teaspoon vinegar

Orange, 1 medium	• 6 to 8 tablespoons juice and 2 to 3 tablespoons grated rind
Mushrooms, 1 pound fresh	• 1 (8-ounce) can sliced mushrooms, drained • 3 ounces dried mushrooms, rehydrated
Onion, chopped, 1 medium	• 1 tablespoon instant minced onion • 1 tablespoon onion powder

Bell pepper
  red or green, chopped, 3 tablespoons
  red, chopped, 3 tablespoons
	• 1 tablespoon dried red or green bell pepper flakes, rehydrated
	• 2 tablespoons diced pimiento

Shallots, chopped, 3 tablespoons	• 2 tablespoons chopped onion and 1 tablespoon chopped garlic

Tomatoes
  fresh, chopped, 2 cups
  juice, 1 cup
	• 1 (16-ounce) can (may need to drain)
	• ½ cup tomato sauce and ½ cup water

Tomato sauce, 2 cups	• ¾ cup tomato paste and 1 cup water

MISCELLANEOUS

INGREDIENT	SUBSTITUTION
Brandy, 1 tablespoon	• ¼ teaspoon brandy extract and 1 tablespoon water
Broth, beef or chicken canned broth, 1 cup	• 1 bouillon cube dissolved in 1 cup boiling water • 1 cup homemade broth
Chili sauce, 1 cup	• 1 cup tomato sauce, ¼ cup firmly packed brown sugar, 2 tablespoons vinegar, ¼ teaspoon cinnamon, dash of ground cloves, and dash of allspice
Gelatin, flavored, 3-ounce package	• 1 tablespoon unflavored gelatin and 2 cups fruit juice
Honey, 1 cup	• 1¼ cups sugar and ¼ cup water
Ketchup, 1 cup	• 1 cup tomato sauce, ½ cup granulated sugar, and 2 tablespoons white vinegar (for use in cooking)
Macaroni, uncooked, 2 cups (4 cups, cooked)	• 2 cups uncooked spaghetti • 4 cups uncooked egg noodles
Mayonnaise, light, 1 cup (for salads and dressings)	• ½ cup plain fat-free yogurt and ½ cup light mayonnaise • 1 cup low-fat sour cream • 1 cup 1% low-fat cottage cheese pureed in a blender
Rice, uncooked, 1 cup regular (3 cups cooked)	• 1 cup uncooked converted rice • 1 cup uncooked brown rice
Vinegar, balsamic, ½ cup	• ½ cup red wine vinegar (slight flavor difference)

SEASONING PRODUCTS

INGREDIENT	SUBSTITUTION
Allspice, ground, 1 teaspoon	• ½ teaspoon ground cinnamon and ½ teaspoon ground cloves
Chives, fresh, chopped, 1 tablespoon	• 1 tablespoon chopped green onion tops
Garlic, 1 clove, small	• ⅛ teaspoon garlic powder or minced dried garlic
Garlic salt, 1 teaspoon	• ⅛ teaspoon garlic powder and ⅞ teaspoon salt
Herbs, fresh, chopped, 1 tablespoon	• 1 teaspoon dried herbs or ¼ teaspoon ground herbs
Horseradish, fresh, grated, 1 tablespoon	• 2 tablespoons prepared horseradish
Mustard, dried, 1 teaspoon	• 1 tablespoon prepared mustard
Onion powder, 1 tablespoon	• 1 medium onion, chopped • 1 tablespoon instant minced onion
Parsley, dried, 1 teaspoon	• 1 tablespoon chopped fresh parsley
Pimiento, chopped, 2 tablespoons	• 1 tablespoon dried red pepper flakes, rehydrated • 2 to 3 tablespoons chopped red bell pepper
Pumpkin pie spice, 1 teaspoon	• ½ teaspoon ground cinnamon, ¼ teaspoon ground ginger, ⅛ teaspoon ground allspice, and ⅛ teaspoon ground nutmeg
Vanilla bean, 1 (1-inch) piece	• 1 teaspoon vanilla extract
Worcestershire sauce, 1 teaspoon	• 1 teaspoon bottled steak sauce

FOOD	WEIGHT (OR COUNT)	YIELD
Apples	1 pound (3 medium)	3 cups sliced
Bananas	1 pound (3 medium)	2½ cups sliced or about 2 cups mashed
Bread	1 pound	12 to 16 slices
	About 1½ slices	1 cup fresh breadcrumbs
Cabbage	1 pound head	4½ cups shredded
Carrots	1 pound	3 cups shredded
Cheese, American or cheddar	1 pound	About 4 cups shredded
cottage	1 pound	2 cups
cream	3- ounce package	6 tablespoons
Chocolate chips	6- ounce package	1 cup
Cocoa	1 pound	4 cups
Coconut, flaked or shredded	1 pound	5 cups
Coffee	1 pound	80 tablespoons (40 cups perked)
Corn	2 medium ears	1 cup kernels
Cornmeal	1 pound	3 cups
Crab, in shell	1 pound	¾ to 1 cup flaked
Crackers, chocolate wafers	19 wafers	1 cup crumbs
graham crackers	14 squares	1 cup crumbs
saltine crackers	28 crackers	1 cup crumbs
vanilla wafers	22 wafers	1 cup crumbs
Dates, pitted	1 pound	3 cups chopped
	8- ounce package	1½ cups chopped
Eggs	4 large	1 cup
whites	8 to 11	1 cup
yolks	12 to 14	1 cup
Flour, all-purpose	1 pound	3½ cups
cake	1 pound	4¾ to 5 cups sifted
whole-wheat	1 pound	3½ cups unsifted
Green bell pepper	1 large	1 cup diced
Lemon	1 medium	2 to 3 tablespoons juice; 2 teaspoons grated rind
Lettuce	1- pound head	6¼ cups torn
Lime	1 medium	1½ to 2 tablespoons juice; 1½ teaspoons grated rind
Macaroni	4 ounces dry (1 cup)	2 cups cooked
Margarine	1 pound	2 cups
	¼- pound stick	½ cup
Marshmallows	10 large	1 cup
	10 miniature	1 large marshmallow
	½ pound miniature	4½ cups
Milk, evaporated, skim	12- ounce can	1½ cups

FOOD	WEIGHT (OR COUNT)	YIELD
Milk, continued		
sweetened, condensed, fat-free		
or low-fat	14- ounce can	1¼ cups
Mushrooms	3 cups raw (8 ounces)	1 cup sliced cooked
Nuts, almonds	1 pound	1 to 1¾ cups nutmeats
	1 pound shelled	3½ cups nutmeats
peanuts	1 pound	2¼ cups nutmeats
	1 pound shelled	3 cups
pecans	1 pound	2¼ cups nutmeats
	1 pound shelled	4 cups
walnuts	1 pound	1⅔ cups nutmeats
	1 pound shelled	4 cups
Oats, quick-cooking	1 cup	1¾ cups cooked
Onion	1 medium	½ cup chopped
Orange	1 medium	½ cup juice; 2 tablespoons grated rind
Peaches	2 medium	1 cup sliced
Pears	2 medium	1 cup sliced
Potatoes, baking	3 medium	2 cups cubed cooked or 1¾ cups mashed
sweet	3 medium	3 cups sliced
Raisins	1 pound	3 cups
Rice, long-grain	1 cup	3 to 4 cups cooked
quick-cooking	1 cup	2 cups cooked
Shrimp, raw in shell	1½ pounds	2 cups (¾ pound) cleaned, cooked
Spaghetti	7 ounces	About 4 cups cooked
Strawberries	1 quart	4 cups sliced
Sugar, brown	1 pound	2⅓ cups firmly packed
powdered	1 pound	3½ cups unsifted
granulated	1 pound	2 cups

EQUIVALENT MEASURES

3 teaspoons	1	tablespoon	2 cups....................	1	pint (16 fluid ounces)
4 tablespoons	¼	cup	4 cups....................	1	quart
5⅓ tablespoons	⅓	cup	4 quarts	1	gallon
8 tablespoons	½	cup	⅛ cup	2	tablespoons
16 tablespoons	1	cup	⅓ cup	5	tablespoons plus 1 teaspoon
2 tablespoons (liquid)	1	ounce	⅔ cup	10	tablespoons plus 2 teaspoons
1 cup.....................................	8	fluid ounces	¾ cup	12	tablespoons

amaretto An almond-flavored liqueur often made with the kernels of apricot pits.

anchovy paste A combination of ground anchovy fillets, vinegar, spices, and water that is packaged in tubes.

balsamic vinegar An Italian vinegar made from white Trebbiano grapes. Aged over a period of years in wooden barrels, the vinegar has a dark color and pungent sweetness.

Bundt pan A tube pan with fluted sides.

cake flour A soft-wheat flour with a fine texture and high starch content used to produce very tender cakes and pastries.

cooking apples Apples that remain firm and flavorful when cooked, such as Baldwin, Cortland, Granny Smith, Northern Spy, Rome Beauty, Winesap, and York Imperial.

custard cup A small deep-sided, individual glass baking dish similar to a ramekin.

gratin dish A round or oval ovenproof dish with shallow sides, allowing more area for surface crisping.

Gruyère cheese A firm, yellow cow's-milk cheese with medium-size holes, named after a valley in Switzerland.

julienne To cut into thin matchlike strips, especially vegetables.

kirsch A colorless, unaged brandy distilled from cherry juice and pits.

leek Similar in appearance to a giant scallion, the leek has a cylindrical white bulb and flat, dark-green leaves. The flavor is reminiscent of those of garlic and onion but milder and more subtle.

mixed peppercorns A combination of black, white, pink, and freeze-dried green peppercorns.

Neufchâtel cheese A soft, white, unripened cheese similar to cream cheese.

papaya A golden-skinned, pear-shaped tropical fruit with juicy, smooth yellow-orange flesh and an exotic sweet-tart flavor. The large center cavity is packed with shiny, grayish-black seeds that are edible but usually discarded.

pesto An uncooked sauce usually made with basil that has been ground together with pine nuts, garlic, olive oil, and cheese. Other herbs such as cilantro and mint may be substituted.

raspberry vinegar A fruit vinegar made by steeping raspberries in vinegar.

rice vinegar A mild and slightly sweet vinegar made from fermented rice.

rosé wine Also called blush wine, a rosé is made from red grapes, but the skins and stems are removed almost immediately. This produces a pale-pink, light-bodied, slightly sweet wine.

rye flour A heavy, dark-colored flour milled from cereal grass, which produces dark, dense loaves of bread. Because of its low gluten (protein) content, it performs best when used in combination with higher-protein flour such as all-purpose.

savory An herb of the mint family with two varieties, summer and winter. Summer savory is slightly milder than winter savory, but both have a strong flavor reminiscent of a cross between thyme and mint.

self-rising flour A blend of all-purpose flour, baking powder, and salt.

sesame oil An oil expressed from sesame seeds. Sesame oil comes in two basic types: light and dark. The light is yellow in color with a mild nutty flavor; the dark has a much stronger flavor and fragrance. This mahogany-colored oil is frequently used in Asian dishes.

shallot A plant related to the onion but formed with a divided bulb like garlic. The shallot has a mild onion flavor.

watercress Part of the mustard family, this plant grows in clear, running streams and has pungent-tasting leaves often used in salads and soups and as a garnish.

wheat germ The embryo of the wheat kernel, wheat germ is a concentrated source of vitamins, minerals, and protein. It is sold in both toasted and natural form and has a nutty flavor.

zest The aromatic, colored portion of the skin (and not the white pith) of citrus fruit.

Nutrition and Serving-Size Information

Here are some specific guidelines *Weight Watchers* Magazine adheres to regarding our recipes. For nutritional accuracy, please follow our suggestions.

• When preparing a recipe that yields more than one serving, it is important to mix the ingredients well and then divide the mixture evenly.

• Where liquid and solid parts have to be divided evenly, drain the liquid and set it aside. Evenly divide the remaining ingredients; then add equal amounts of the liquid to each serving.

• Unless otherwise indicated, selections of meat, poultry, and fish refer to cooked, skinned, and boned servings.

• The selection information is designated as follows: P/M (Protein/Milk), FA (Fat), FR/V (Fruit/Vegetable), B (Bread), C (Bonus Calories).

• The selection information no longer contains fractions: B, FR/V, and FA are rounded up if 0.5 or above; P/M is rounded up if 0.75 or above; and C only includes bonus calories above 30. If all of the selections are rounded up, bonus calories are decreased; if all of the selections are rounded down, bonus calories are increased.

• Recipes also provide approximate nutritional data, including the following: cal (calories), pro (protein), fat (total fat), sat (saturated fat), carb (carbohydrates), fib (dietary fiber), chol (cholesterol), iron (iron), sod (sodium), calc (calcium). Measurements are abbreviated as follows: g (grams), mg (milligrams).

Note: Because data on fat distribution are not available for some processed foods, these breakdowns should be considered approximate.

• Recipes include *POINTS*™ based on Weight Watchers International's 1•2•3 Success™ Weight Loss Plan. (Please turn to page 3 for more information about this plan.)

• *POINTS* are calculated from a formula based on calories, fat, and fiber that assigns higher points to higher-calorie, higher-fat foods. Based on your present weight, you are allowed a certain amount of *POINTS* per day.

• The recipes that are shown in our photographs may vary as to the number of servings pictured. It is important that you refer to the recipes for the exact serving information.

U S E F U L   E Q U I V A L E N T S   F O R   L I Q U I D   I N G R E D I E N T S   B Y   V O L U M E

	Fahrenheit	Celsius	Gas Mark
Freeze Water	32° F	0°C	
Room Temperature	68° F	20° C	
Boil Water	212° F	100° C	
Bake	325° F	160° C	3
	350° F	180° C	4
	375° F	190° C	5
	400° F	200° C	6
	425° F	220° C	7
	450° F	230° C	8
Broil			Grill

Anew Perfect Cleanser
The first step of any Anew treatment. Exceptionally mild formula is less drying than ordinary soap.

Anew Perfecting Lotion for Problem Skin
Age-fighting alpha hydroxy formula containing salicylic acid. Helps prevent acne blemishes.

Anew Alpha Peel-Off Facial Mask
Combines botanicals with an alpha hydroxy formula to deliver younger-looking skin in 10 minutes. Refines and conditions.

Anew Perfect Eye Care Cream
Moisturizes and nourishes delicate undereye area. Improves appearance of fine lines and wrinkles within weeks.

Anew All-in-One Intensive Complex
Twice the concentration of AHA found in Anew Perfecting Complex. With moisturizers, antioxidants and SPF 15. Smooths, hydrates, protects.

Dare to change your mind about avon.

Anew Formula C Facial Treatment
Pure Vitamin C delivered directly to the skin. Improves skin clarity. Helps skin look firmer.

Anew All-in-One Perfecting Lotion
New light, oil-free lotion. Age-fighting AHA formula with moisturizers, antioxidants, and SPF 8. Smooths, hydrates, protects.

Anew All-in-One Perfecting Complex
The advanced alpha hydroxy formula. With moisturizers, antioxidants and SPF 15. Smooths, hydrates, protects.

Anew Skincare.
Advanced technology in a line of breakthrough products designed for maximum benefits for all skin types. Satisfaction guaranteed or your money back. Dare to change your mind about Avon.
Call your Avon Representative, visit Avon at www.avon.com or order direct

1-800-FOR-AVON

A V O N